ON NEW-BLOWN ROSES

Spring, and the sharpness of the golden dawn.
Before the sun was up a cooler breeze
Had blown, in promise of a day of heat,
And I was walking in my formal garden,
To freshen me, before the day grew old.

I saw the hoar frost stiff on the bent grasses,
Sitting in fat globes on the cabbage leaves,
And all my Paestum roses laughing at me,
Dew-drenched, and in the East the morning star,
And here and there a dewdrop glistening white,
That soon must perish in the early sun.

Think you, did Dawn steal colour from the roses,
Or was it new-born day that stained the rose?
To each one dew, one crimson and one morning,
To star and rose, their lady Venus one.
Mayhap one fragrance, but the sweet of Dawn
Drifts through the sky, and closer breathes the rose.

A moment dies; this bud that was new-born
Has burgeoned even fold on even fold;
This still is green with her close cap of leaves,
This shows a red stain on her tender sheath,
This the first crimson of the loosened bud.

And now she thinks to unwind her coverings,
And lo! the glory of the radiant chalice,
Scatt'ring the close seeds of her golden heart.
One moment, all on fire and crimson glowing,
All pallid now and bare and desolate,
I marvelled at the flying rape of time;
But now a rose was born; that rose is old.
Even as I speak the crimson petals float
Down drifting, and the crimsoned earth is bright.

So many lovely things, so rare, so young,
A day begat them, and a day will end.
O Earth, to give a flower so brief a grace!
As long as a day is long, so long the life of a rose.
The golden sun at morning sees her born,
And late at eve returning finds her old.
Yet wise is she, that hath so soon to die,
And lives her life in some succeeding rose.
O maid, while youth is with the rose and thee,
Pluck thou the rose; life is as swift for thee.

The old retired Roman civil servant Ausonius wrote this poem
400 years before the birth of Christ.

CYRIL FLETCHER'S

Rose Book

WITH PHOTOGRAPHS BY MICHAEL WARREN A.I.I.P.

Collins

To my wife who, like all good roses
is even more beautiful in her maturity.

How Roses are Named

For those of us to whom gardening is a hobby and fun, the naming of plants seems to be almost a complicated science on its own. I do not want to be too technical in this book—it is more for our delight than our instruction. However, we must make ourselves clear over a few terms, if you don't mind.

All roses belong to the genus *Rosa*. The genus is divided into species—for example, the Dog rose is the species *Rosa canina*. In turn, each species may have several varieties: these can be botanical varieties, or garden varieties or cultivars. Thus we have:

Genus: *Rosa*   Species: *Rosa canina*   Variety: *Rosa Canina andersonii*

Clones are a group of individuals derived originally from a single individual— as 'Chicago Peace' was derived from 'Peace'. Then there are the Hybrids, which are crosses between varieties, subspecies and species. There are bi-generic hybrids . . . do you want me to go on?

Anyway to make your life easier and the reading of this book more enjoyable, what we have done is as follows: we have printed the genus and species names, and the names of botanical varieties, in italics, and the names of cultivars (garden varieties) with capital letters in quotation marks. Hence *Rosa rugosa* and *R. rugosa alba*, but 'Agnes' and 'Roseraie de l'Hay'.

From time to time names are changed by the authorities. The RHS tells us that 'there are three distinct causes of name changes: misidentifications, nomenclatural errors, and taxonomic revisions'. All of this is important because proper naming of the myriad forms and kinds of plants enables them to be discussed, bought and bred with certainty and clarity. We are grateful to the learned botanists who do this for us, but at the same time confused and a little irritated that a plant known for years as 'Creeping Marmalade' has become something quite unpronounceable.

First published in 1983
by William Collins Sons & Co. Ltd
London and Glasgow
9 8 7 6 5 4 3 2 1

© text Cyril Fletcher 1983

ISBN 0 00 410435 8 (hardback)
ISBN 0 00 410434 X (paperback)

Printed in Britain by
William Collins Sons & Co. Ltd

Contents

INTRODUCTION
page 7

I

HISTORY OF THE ROSE
page 8

2

HOW TO GROW ROSES
page 20

3

CLIMBING & RAMBLER ROSES—AND ROSES FOR HEDGES
page 30

4

ROSES FOR GROUND COVER—AND GROUND COVER FOR ROSES
page 40

5

HYBRID TEAS, FLORIBUNDAS AND MINIATURE ROSES
page 48

6

OLD SHRUB ROSES
page 60

7

BREEDING A NEW ROSE
page 70

8

PLANNING A ROSE GARDEN
page 76

9

FAMOUS ROSE GARDENS
page 92

10

THE ROYAL NATIONAL ROSE SOCIETY
page 108

L'ENVOI
page 123

INDEX
page 124

ACKNOWLEDGEMENTS
page 128

May'st thou long, sweet crimson gem,
Richly deck thy native stem;
Till some evening, sober, calm,
Dropping dews, and breathing balm,
While all around the woodland rings,
And every bird thy requiem sings;
Thou amid the dirgeful sound,
Shed thy dying honours round,
And resign to Parent Earth,
The loveliest form she e'er gave birth.
ROBERT BURNS, 1759–1796

Photograph of 'Tuscany Superb'

Introduction

You may be a very experienced gardener, but for the moment I want to imagine that you have not long come to gardening; a newly keen amateur. You have begun to realize the value of plants, so that you will especially value one that blooms for a long period, is hardy and fragrant, will live a long time, and is not so rare as to make it hard to come by or too expensive. Shrubs are good in this way; they have longevity, they do not need staking, they are often floriferous for a time and fragrant too.

Now I am going to recommend a shrub which comes in several forms: it is low-growing, it can be climbing, it can be a standard or a miniature, it can be a hybrid or a species. It comes in every colour, white, yellow, orange, vermilion and crimson to darkest red, sometimes with a trace of lavender-blue. Most of them flower at least twice in the season, some of them on and off throughout the whole season. The perfume from the flowers is glorious—and in some cases the foliage is scented too. Perfumes have been made from them for centuries—when the flowers are dead they can be strewn for emperors to wade through, the petals can be used to pelt a bride, candied they can be eaten, or they can be fermented into a potent wine. The seed-pods are decorative, and can also be used to make a vitaminized drink. Amongst its many uses in the garden this shrub can fill a formal bed, clothe a wall, hide a gasworks, provide ground cover, or climb up and into a tree and throw itself from the topmost branches in fragrant garlands of exotic colours down to earth again.

In addition to all these virtues, because so many people are devoted to and delighted by this wonder shrub, breeders all over the world are producing new varieties, new colours and new hardiness. There is a Royal National Society to inform, instruct and enthuse, and to conduct trials for all the new coming varieties.

Having seen the title of the book and the picture on the cover you will have guessed by now that this marvel of the garden is The Rose, in all its forms and all its glories.

The Rose is surely the Queen of Flowers. It is a flower apart. There is a wonder about it. Pick an opening bud of a 'Papa Meilland' rose: it is the darkest of reds, and in its innermost recesses it is a shadowy black. Breathe in its perfume: it is velvet to touch and velvet-scented on the air. Next to your skin it is velvet again—no, it is veined satin. It is best to make this appraisal in the evening, an incense laden summer evening, the air close and the sun redly setting in the west. This rose suddenly has your undivided attention. Has it a secret to unfold? A message to deliver? This is a distillation from the earth. This is beauty. 'A sudden gladness gleams on the soul,' wrote Coleridge. You will have shared a magical spiritual experience with the essence of the garden. A rose is more than just a flower. It brings with it a glimmer of the whys and wherefores of Creation. There must be an inner meaning to the mystery of their loveliness.

Cyril Fletcher

1

History of the Rose

Sweet June, sweet Sussex and the sun. Not a day to laze, but a day of blue sky and high cloud; the wind a caress. We would drive into the Weald of England. When you talk of Sussex and Kent, the White Cliffs of Dover immediately come to mind—Albion, but Albion, we like to think, was called after the Alba rose, a native of this blessed land and cherished since Roman times. One thinks too of the rolling downs of Sussex, the grass tumbled with windy currents, like the sea, with quickly passing shadows from high argosies of sail-like cloud. One does not immediately think of that vast heart of forest from which the ships were built which conquered the Armada, the staunch land of the Hobdens, the tillers of Wealden clay, whose patriotic obstinacy was extolled by Kipling who lived there and loved the soil, the stone and the ancient English core of the place so dearly.

This was where we would go on this favoured day where all of nature, smiling in the sun, was forgetful of the frost and snow and fog and lashing rain that had brought to fruition the beauty of this Garden of England, as the Weald is called. And we were to go to the very heart of it, along the tiny leafy lanes, at the crown of the year and to the crown of the gardener's art—to Sissinghurst to see the roses. In this June, the month of scents and sounds, the murmuring of doves and bees, the call of the lazy cuckoo and the warm scent of mown grass enveloped us; the roses over the cottage doors enchanted us. 'All beauty in a little world may be, though the roof lean and muddy be the floor.' Then, suddenly, there was the Tower, the ancient red brick centre. In the 1930s this had been surrounded by nettles and briars, docks and old bedsteads—the rubbish of careless villagers. Here Vita Sackville-West, writer and poetess, was to plant and to cherish a garden which was to be even more lyrical than her poems, and which would give her a fame that perhaps her

---

Right: Arching over an ancient urn, in the centre of the White Garden at Sissinghurst, *Rosa filipes* 'Kiftsgate' left us speechless.

carefully pruned and tended words would not have done. Here she poetically practised what she called 'Agriculture's little brother'.

In her poem 'The Garden', she writes: 'Much soil, much love and many years went to the slow reward.' And later: 'and might be disappointed to arrive'. This we are not.

The sun for centuries has warmed these walls—walls of Kentish ragstone and of bricks—bricks which the Tudors had made, and built with. This was the perfect setting. I know of none better for seeing the old roses—which Miss Sackville-West called then the 'old-fashionable roses'. She writes: 'Visitors who look among the roses for the hybrid-tea and perpetuals will be disappointed.' These ancient walls shelter and contain the sprawling exuberant habit of the old roses—the Gallicas, Musks, Damasks and Cabbages (Centifolia roses)—and the way they are contained within the box and yew hedges and the brick paths, without pruning, some mingling into each other, is a marvellous example of controlled disarray.

Here to cover the wall of South Cottage was the rose 'Mme Alfred Carrière', several hundred square feet of it; the very vigorous climber with flowers the palest blush pink, incense-scented and abundant-flowering.

Over a doorway into the courtyard were the lovely cabbage shapes of the blossoms of 'Paul's Lemon Pillar'. It is really white, but there is a trace of lemon at its heart, and so strangely scented as one passes underneath.

She found a charming old Gallica growing at Sissinghurst—a dark velvety one, not unlike 'Tuscany'; it is extremely floriferous and grows on a stiff stem suitable for cutting. Was Miss Sackville-West thinking of this rose when she wrote:

> She's a voluptuary; think of her
> Wine-dark and heavy-scented of the South,.
> Stuck in a cap or dangled from a mouth
> As soft as her own petals. That's the rose!

'Felicia' scented the air luxuriantly. This is one of the Hybrid Musk roses raised by the Revd Joseph Pemberton.

There was a long walk bordered by Pemberton hybrids (the Hybrid Musks)—'Danae', 'Penelope', 'Cornelia', 'Felicia', 'Thisbe'—and these scented the air luxuriantly. In the orchard, throwing themselves over the trees and hanging down like fountains of blossom, were the species roses, the Sweet briars, *Rosa filipes* 'Kiftsgate', *R. longicuspis* from western China, and 'Paul's Himalayan Musk' rambler, with small, scented, double flowers of blush pink.

Leaving the rose garden and crossing the Tower Lawn, suddenly we came into the White Garden. We were speechless; the whole poetic confection of white and grey and green and silver was very lovely. In the centre of this garden, arching over an ancient leaden urn, was *R. filipes* 'Kiftsgate' at its very best, its flowers airborne in panicles of perhaps twenty dainty white flowers with bright yellow anthers. We saw this huge mound of fragrant clusters of white flowers against a blue sky—a pageant of a plant!

This lovely garden, heart of the English Weald, gave me my first love of roses—not just the old ones, though perhaps they give me the most delight—and because of the pleasure this passion gives to

me, I have a desire to share it with all gardeners who care to read. That is the reason for this book, and the ensuing chapters. Let us now try and trace the history of this enchanting flower.

'Celsiana': here is the beauty of the Damask rose.

*   *   *

You cannot imagine seventy million years. But all that time ago four-petalled roses basked in the sun. How do we know? Fossils of roses have been found in Europe, Asia and America, all in the northern hemisphere. There they are for us to see, clearly imprinted in stone, ancient and inviolate.

We know so little of the origin of man's different races, and we know still less of how all the different species of roses began. We are told that they started like our own Dog roses, single and innocent, and according to the effect of their environment on them—be it hot, cold, windy, stony or luxuriant—so the rose developed one way or the other. There might have been 200 different kinds of wild roses—the animals and the winds, and eventually man, spread them and nature married each to each, and various forms in various parts of the world evolved.

The rose has its roots as firmly in the history of civilization as it has in the gardens of the world. The garden rose has come to us from China, Persia, Japan and the Himalayas, and from the native Dog

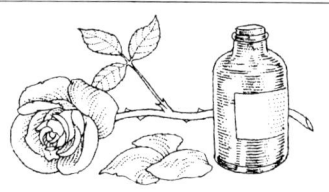

SOME USES FOR ROSE PETALS

Tepid rose water is good for bathing tired eyes, especially when used half and half with witch hazel. To make rose water pour a cupful of the petals of red roses like 'Ernest H. Morse', 'Josephine Bruce', 'Papa Meilland' or 'Wendy Cussons' into $\frac{1}{2}$ pint (250ml) boiling water. Cover and leave for an hour, then strain into bottles and cork tightly.

*   *   *

If you want to scent your linen, dry rose petals on sheets of paper in the sun or in an airing cupboard and use in bags. The rose petals can be used on their own or with lavender and sweet marjoram.

Opposite: *R. alba semi-plena*: the rose that inspired the Renaissance painters.

rose of England's hedgerows, too. Religions have worshipped it, nations have used it as their emblem, and poets have sung its praises endlessly. ('Grows' rhymes rather too easily with 'rose'!)

It is thought that China may have been the first place where man brought the rose into his garden. Chinese garden culture commenced around 3,000 years BC—ignoring the odd year or two! Confucius—that great Chinese comedy script writer!—writes of extensive rose plantings in Peking 500 years before Christ. Roses were also cultivated very early in the Middle East, having been brought wild from China and India.

It would seem that man has needed the companionship of the rose—like the dog—from his earliest beginnings. The first known depictions of roses are from the frescoes of the great Minoan Palace of Knossos in Crete 2,000 years BC, but roses were used in the religious ceremonies of the Median fire-worshippers as far back as the twelfth century BC. When the royal graves of Ur of the Chaldes were excavated, Sir Leonard Woolley discovered that 5,000 years ago the Sumerian King Sargon brought roses back to his country as battle plunder. Incidentally, there are only two mentions of roses in the whole of the Bible.

The ancient Greeks used roses to prophesy: they clapped the rose petals against their hands and, according to the noise made, they were able to divine the future.

The Romans used rose water to perfume their clothes—and even their shoe leather. Petals fell from the ceilings like snow on Nero and his guests. The palanquins the Emperor's ladies were carried around in had cushions stuffed with rose petals. We are told that when Cleopatra met Mark Anthony in Sicily in 42 BC the floor of the banqueting chamber was covered in roses two feet deep. So she didn't exactly rush into his arms, did she? The Romans had hot houses called *specularia* where hot water circulated in earthenware pipes, so cut roses were available all the year round.

Pliny, the great Roman encyclopaedist, listed thirty-two medicines which could be prepared from roses. Most of these were evolved from rose water, oil of roses, and syrup of roses. Those of us old enough to remember the last war will remember how rose hip syrup provided the young members of the nation with their vitamin C. It is still widely sold for babies today.

The Dark Ages were a sad time with hardly a rose to lighten them. In the eighth century Charlemagne, who passed a law that every home should have a house leek to keep away witches, insisted that lilies and roses should be cultivated as well. The monastery gardens—largely planted for food or with plants of medicinal value—also featured the rose.

The Crusaders, we are told, brought roses home from the wars. The Damask rose they brought to us from the neighbourhood of Damascus. *Rosa gallica*, from which the Damask rose comes, is considered to be the one from which most of our European roses are descended. Thank you Crusaders.

The Apothecary's rose of Provins was *R. gallica officinalis*; in the thirteenth century it was grown round the town of Provins, south-east of Paris. This became the centre of the French rose perfume

'Erinnerung an Brod'
(Hybrid Perpetual).

industry. Around the Balkans and the eastern Mediterranean attar of roses, an essential oil, has been made for hundreds of years. The Kazanlik rose was a Damask rose brought to Bulgaria from Persia in the seventeenth century; there is a flourishing industry there to this day. It takes three tons of flowers to make two pounds of oil! Attar of roses is also made in France and India. It is the essence used in the original sweetmeat called Turkish Delight.

Gerard, the great English herbalist, wrote in his *Herball* in 1597: 'The Rose doth deserve the chief and prime place among all flowers whatsoever, being not onlie esteemed for his beauty, vertues and his fragrant and odiferous smell; but also because it is the honour and ornament of our English Sceptre.' While Culpeper, the seventeenth-century writer on pharmacy, stressed its medicinal properties: 'Of the Red Roses are usually made many compositions, all serving to sundry good uses, viz Electuary of Roses, conserve both moist and dry, which is usually called Sugar of Roses, Syrup of dry Roses and Honey of Roses . . . Honey of Roses is much used in gargles and lotions to wash sores, either in the mouth, throat or other parts, both to cleanse and heal them . . . rose leaves and mint, heated and applied outwardly to the stomach, stay castings and very much strengthen a weak stomach.' An old remedy for lung ailments was to pound red rose petals with sugar and honey in a mortar and take a teaspoonful three times a day.

In 1731 there was published *The Gardener's Dictionary*, which lists forty-six sorts of rose. John H. Harvey, gardener and author of *Early Gardening Catalogues* (Phillimore, 1972) and *Early Nurserymen* (Phillimore, 1975), writes with great authority of the old gardening catalogues. He tells us that the best sources of information about roses in the eighteenth century are the surviving nurserymen's catalogues, and old bills sent to purchasers for the supply of plants. There is also William Aiton's *Hortus Kewensis*, published in 1789. In it Aiton, principal gardener at Kew, recorded the dates when exotic species reached Kew. 'The Twelve Months of Flowers' was a magnificently illustrated catalogue published by a Kensington nurseryman, Robert Furber.

Then chronologically there is a host of catalogues followed by Miss Mary Lawrance's famous book *A Collection of Roses from Nature*, published in 1799, with ninety hand-coloured enlargements. (The dwarf *R. lawranceana*, syn. *R. chinensis minima*, was named after her—also an early red rose, which was called 'Gloire de Lawranceanas' in 1837.)

In 1799, Napoleon Bonaparte bought a dilapidated property—an old sanatorium for tuberculous patients—called La Malmaison, for the Empress Josephine. This was her retreat from the bustle of the Court, and here she made a garden famous for its roses. It was her aim to collect every possible variety of rose then in existence. In all there were over 250 different roses, species, sports of species, and hybrids—though not of course intentional hybrids, for specialist rose growers at that time were few and far between. She also became the patron of Pierre-Joseph Redouté, the famous Belgian flower painter. She retired to La Malmaison after her divorce.

I am not going to go in any great detail into the history of all the

HOW TO MAKE ROSE PETAL WINE
by Domini Gregory

Of all the wines I make, this is the most difficult to perfect, due to the fact that only fresh, red, perfumed petals ('Deep Secret', 'Alec's Red', 'Mr Lincoln', 'Papa Meilland', etc.) are used and nothing else is added to give body. If this were done the delicacy of colour and fragrance would be overpowered by the other ingredients. Please use the petals as soon as possible as they are highly perishable. They may be refrigerated for 2–3 days. Available in Sweet, Medium and occasionally Dry.

The following are the ingredients for 1 gallon (4½ litres) of Rose Petal Wine (this being the equivalent of six normal bottles):

1lb (450g) rose petals (they must be dry)
2½lb (1.1kg) white sugar (this amount will make a medium-sweet wine)
Juice of 2 lemons or 1 tbsp. powdered citric acid (I only use citric acid—lemon flavours too much)
1 gallon (4½ litres) water
Yeast (wine yeast if possible, or 1 tsp. dried)
Yeast nutrient (add with the yeast—1 tsp. or 1 tablet)
½lb (225g) chopped raisins (optional—they will give added body)

First put a funnel in the neck of a jar. (A glass demi-john with 'ears' is the most suitable, and may be obtained from most good wine-making shops.) Pour the sugar through the funnel into the jar, together with the lemon juice or citric acid.

Boil the water in a large preserving pan or enamel bucket, and add all the rose petals, boiling them for about 15 minutes (with the chopped raisins, if used). When the liquid has cooled strain it through muslin or linen into the jar, stirring to dissolve the sugar.

When this liquid has cooled to about 70°F (21°C) add the yeast and yeast nutrient, either on its own or creamed with a little of the lukewarm liquid. Fit an airlock, or stuff cottonwool in the neck of the jar, then put the vessel in a warm place and allow to ferment. When the fermentation has slowed down (approx. 5–6 weeks) syphon the wine off the sediment (lees) into a clean jar and refit airlock.

When the process of fermentation has completely finished, 2–3 months or even longer, the wine should have cleared itself, but if not, it may be filtered. It is now ready to be bottled, but do try and be patient, it *is* worthwhile!!! *Leave this wine, if you can, for about 6 months before drinking.*

(Domini Gregory, who is the wife of Tony Gregory of the famous Nottingham rose nurseries, has made this wine for some years, and I have been the happy recipient of a bottle many times.)

MY WIFE BETTY'S ROSE RECIPES

Rose Tea

Take a handful of crimson rose petals and infuse them in a cup of boiling water; if you have a sweet tooth add half a teaspoonful of honey. Jasmine tea is made of tea leaves flavoured with jasmine flowers. A stronger tea can be made of tea leaves and flavoured with rose petals.

Crystallized rose leaves

These can be made in two ways (decisions!). Beat the white of an egg, dip each petal into the egg white, sprinkle with castor sugar, and dry in the sun on the kitchen windowsill on greaseproof paper. The other way is to boil $\frac{1}{2}$lb (225g) sugar in $\frac{1}{4}$ pint (125ml) of water, dip the petals singly into the liquid when the liquid is clear and simmering (for goodness sake be careful as you can easily get blistered fingers!), then dry on greaseproof paper as before. Rose cream chocolates I find delicious, and not least the crystallized petals on top of each one. As I like beer as well (not with chocolates!) what chance have I of a sylph-like figure!

old roses—indeed I am not sufficiently knowledgeable to do so—but as a guide I will now define all the various kinds for you—the Centifolias, the Albas, the Rugosas, and so on. From these definitions please then find your way about. In explaining how each kind came about I have been greatly helped by that master rosarian Michael Gibson, and his authoritative, delightful book *Shrub Roses for Every Garden* (Collins, 1973).

The Gallica Roses These are some of the very oldest roses in cultivation. They have scented blossoms ranging from deepest maroon in colour to pale pink. As we have seen, *R. gallica officinalis* was known as the Apothecary's rose. It was also the red rose of Lancaster. The Gallica makes a smallish, compact shrub which readily suckers, so there is no need to prune.

The Damask Roses *R. damascena* first appeared in England in the sixteenth century or possibly even earlier. Damasks usually have greyish, downy foliage. The Wars of the Roses we all recall from our history books, and how they were brought to an end by the famous rose of red and white—the York and Lancaster rose, a symbol of reconciliation. This was a Damask (not to be confused with 'Rosa Mundi', which is a Gallica)—though the story is probably apocryphal, as there is no evidence that the rose was known in England until many years later. Damask roses have a distinctive perfume. The Portland Damasks repeat flower in the autumn.

The Alba Roses An ancient rose grown by the Greeks and Romans, thought to have come from a cross between the Damask rose and the Dog rose. Albas are often featured in the pictures of the Renaissance painters. They flower in summer, with white, semi-double, scented blooms. The white rose of York and the Jacobite rose were Albas. Another Alba was 'Great Maiden's Blush', as the Victorians called it—but the French, no doubt to Mrs Whitehouse's dismay, called it '*Cuisse de Nymphe Emue*'—or thigh of the passionate nymph. An unusual rose you will agree!

The Centifolia (or Cabbage) Roses Roses of a hundred petals (not leaves, as the name suggests),voluptuous old roses, open, prickly and lax in growth; the outer petals are large and enfold the shorter, tightly packed centre ones. They are not often recurrent but they are beautifully fragrant. 'Fantin-Latour' is a Centifolia, and to me one of the most beautiful of the old roses—with pale pink flowers, very double, and growing in clusters. The Centifolia was also known as the '*Rose des Peintres*' because it so often featured in the old Dutch flower pictures.

The Moss Roses These are usually Centifolias. They are mostly scented, and come in all colours. The buds and stems are dense with a moss-like, glandular, bristly covering which is sticky to the touch, and gives off a resinous, balm-like odour when bruised. Some are recurrent.

The China Roses These first appeared in the West towards the end of the eighteenth century. They flower from the beginning of June until well into the autumn. This asset was quickly recognized by the

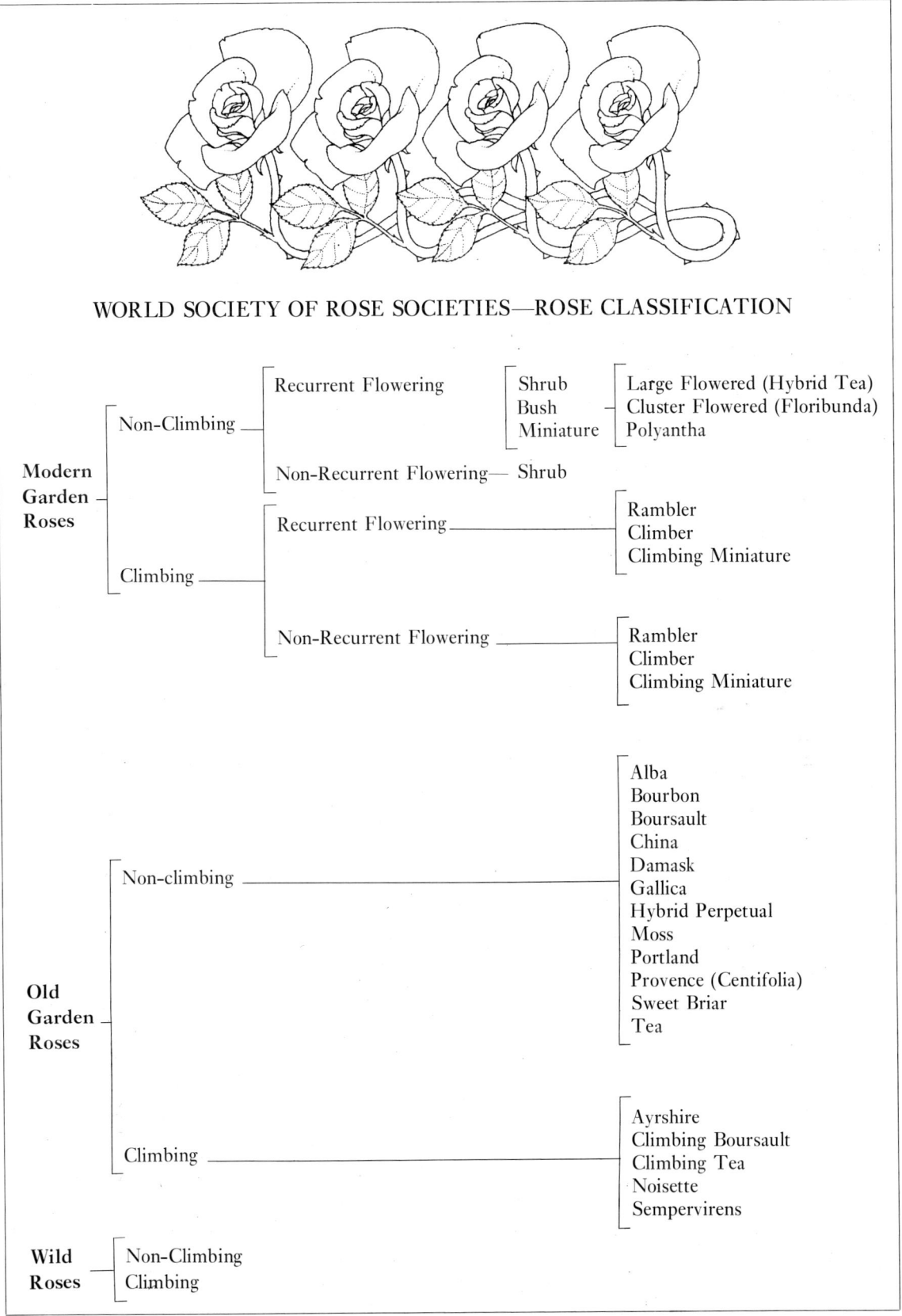

WORLD SOCIETY OF ROSE SOCIETIES—ROSE CLASSIFICATION

Modern Garden Roses
- Non-Climbing
  - Recurrent Flowering
    - Shrub / Bush / Miniature
      - Large Flowered (Hybrid Tea)
      - Cluster Flowered (Floribunda)
      - Polyantha
  - Non-Recurrent Flowering — Shrub
- Climbing
  - Recurrent Flowering
    - Rambler
    - Climber
    - Climbing Miniature
  - Non-Recurrent Flowering
    - Rambler
    - Climber
    - Climbing Miniature

Old Garden Roses
- Non-climbing
  - Alba
  - Bourbon
  - Boursault
  - China
  - Damask
  - Gallica
  - Hybrid Perpetual
  - Moss
  - Portland
  - Provence (Centifolia)
  - Sweet Briar
  - Tea
- Climbing
  - Ayrshire
  - Climbing Boursault
  - Climbing Tea
  - Noisette
  - Sempervirens

Wild Roses
- Non-Climbing
- Climbing

'Fantin-Latour' (Centifolia). For me this is one of the most beautiful old roses, and much liked also by the painter after whom it was named.

rose breeders, and accounts for many of our perpetual flowering roses today. 'Perle d'Or' has an apricot tinge, and *R. semperflorens* is the original dark crimson China rose. These roses form angular bushes, seldom bigger than 4 feet (1.2m).

The Bourbon Roses The accidental crossing of a China rose with the Autumn Damask on the Isle du Bourbon produced the Bourbon roses. The joy of them is that they will flower in June/July and then again (sometimes even better) in September. They were very popular in the second half of the nineteenth century. They have great variety in colour and form.

The Hybrid Perpetual Roses These followed the Bourbons in popularity with the Victorians. All give a second show of bloom in the autumn. The flowers are large, cupped or globular—'Roger Lambelin' has crimson, white-edged, scalloped petals.

The Noisette Roses A Frenchman, Philippe Noisette, in America crossed perpetual flowering China roses with *R. moschata* (the Musk rose) at the beginning of the nineteenth century—hence the Noisette roses. Painted by Redouté, they are mostly climbers, but not very hardy.

The Tea Roses These beautiful Chinese roses are usually grown in greenhouses and conservatories. Some of the hardier ones can be grown out of doors in a sheltered position.

The Rugosa Roses Imported from China and Japan in 1796, the Rugosa is a vigorous perpetual flowering rose with large, rough-textured leaves composed of five to nine downy leaflets. The flowers are fragrant and followed by red tomato-shaped heps. There are both double and single varieties. The flowers are usually pink to maroon, but *alba* and 'Blanc Double de Coubert' are white, and 'Agnes' is yellow. Rugosas are surely the healthiest of all roses.

The Hybrid Musk Roses The original parent of this group, *R. moschata*, the Musk rose, has sweetly scented, creamy white flowers in late summer and autumn. It is richly fragrant. The hybrids were evolved early this century by the Revd Joseph Pemberton. The flowers are borne in large scented clusters, and come in shades of apricot, cream, pale pink, yellow and white. Lilac has been brought in more recently from German breeders. 'Magenta' (1954) has a sweetly scented flower of rosy lilac.

The Hybrid Teas These are the end of the road of the evolution of the rose. The Hybrid Tea originated from the crossing of the Tea rose and the Hybrid Perpetual: the Tea rose was tender and the Hybrid Perpetual vigorous. The first Hybrid Tea to be recognized as such was 'La France', introduced in 1867. Since then the various crossings of this and that rose have been innumerable, and have undoubtedly added to their vigour. The Hybrid Tea is the aristocrat of roses, with its classically shaped bloom—usually a long, pointed bud opening to produce a many-petalled rose with a conical centre.

Another great step forward was the first *yellow* Hybrid Tea. All yellow roses—and from them all the oranges and vermilions too—come from 'Soleil d'Or', first introduced to the public in 1898. A Frenchman Pernet-Ducher, having spent years trying to create a yellow Hybrid Tea-type rose, had given up, but walking one day through his neglected rose fields he found a self-sown seedling with double orange-yellow flowers. I love to try and picture this moment. It must be a little like waiting for the football results and holding the coupon in your shaky excited hand. You have nearly done; your forecast is correct except the last result to come. It comes! You are 100 per cent correct. You throw your hat into the air, possibly your wife's as well. After years of toil, quite by accident you have come across your fortune! Your yellow rose!

The Floribunda Roses Early in the twentieth century the Wichuraiana rambler rose was introduced from Japan and the dwarf Polyantha roses also became popular. The Polyantha roses came from *R. multiflora*; they are short-growing plants with a host of little blooms clustering at the top of the stems. As these were crossed with other roses the flowers became larger and we were on the way to the Floribundas. Poulsen of Denmark, a famous modern rose breeder, established a new kind of rose, the Hybrid Polyantha. The Americans popularized this kind of rose, calling it the Floribunda. Although in many cases the blooms lack the exotic size and beauty of those of the Hybrid Tea, they bear their flowers in large clusters and will flower at least three times a season. Such is their interbreeding with the Hybrid Tea that a completely new kind of rose nomenclature has had to be established (see p. 53).

So, sketchily, that is the long and complicated story of the rose. There is romance in its history. There are dark areas where we have failed to follow its long and devious evolution. The more one knows about the rose, the more mysterious and desirable the quest becomes.

POT-POURRI

For a pot-pourri, that glorious essence of summer which gladdens many a frozen winter heart, gather the roses at their best—just fully open. Put the petals in full sun and then place them in an open ceramic bowl. Sprinkle them with orris root, and in some odd way the inclusion of a few leaves of lemon-scented geranium reinforces the rose perfume. Stir and lightly crush occasionally, not only to bring out the fragrance, but to give you the balm and beneficence of so doing. The quiet, fragrant moment of running your hand through a bowlful of rose petals—particularly if the bowl is aesthetically pleasing too—is the kind of experience which might be assessed in the balance against the snorting aggressive stench of an over-revved motorbike! The gardener and the rose-lover can fortify himself in ways like this to help him to exist today.

2

How to Grow Roses

Thirty-five million new rose trees are bought every year. Some over the counter from supermarkets, some from the local garden centre—either as roots or as pot plants—and some by post, chosen from catalogues. The plant you select may never be more than 4 inches (10cm) high or it may eventually tower 40 feet (12m) into the sky. Let us see what exactly we want for our particular garden, and when we have got it let us check up on how to look after it and ensure that it prospers.

THE DIFFERENT TYPES OF ROSE

Roses come in many different shapes and sizes: first there is the ground cover rose. There are not many kinds to choose from here—some need to be pinned to the ground and some are naturally procumbent. There is a growing need in the modern garden (where labour is expensive and hard to come by and where a good ground-coverer or weed-smotherer is worth its weight (literally) in gold to the gardener) for more ground cover roses; it is my belief that the breeders will do more in this line in the near future. Sam McGredy's 'Snow Carpet' is the first true compact ground cover rose.

The miniature roses come next—hardly ever more than a foot (30cm) high. They look so delicate that one feels they must surely be grown indoors or in a greenhouse but they are as hardy as any other! 'Royal Salute', to celebrate Her Majesty's Silver Jubilee, is a good example: it has fine rose-pink, fragrant, miniature flowers.

There are two kinds of bush rose: the Hybrid Tea and the Floribunda—to use a slightly outdated term—though the hybridizing has now become so complicated between the two kinds of rose that it often requires a specialist grower to know exactly which group claims which. Indeed, there are some which are grouped by different authorities into different categories.

Right: Bob Price took this picture in the Central TV garden at Kings Heath. I am surrounded by 'Nevada', with 'Constance Spry' behind.

Half standard roses are grown on single stems $2\frac{1}{2}$ feet (75cm) high; full standards are $3\frac{1}{2}$ feet (105cm) high, and weeping standards (usually of rambler roses) are on stems 5 feet (1.5m) high. Standards can be Hybrid Teas or Floribundas. There are also miniature standards, about 2 feet (60cm) high. Pillar roses are usually about 8 feet (2.4m), while rambler and climbing roses can grow to anything up to 40 feet (12m).

All roses are shrubs but the ones known as shrub roses are different. They come in all sizes from 2 feet (60cm) tall to 12 feet (3.6m) and some are sufficiently unusual and arresting to be used as focal points in a garden. Their chief disadvantage is that many of them only flower once, but some are repeat flowering, and all have decorative foliage and heps in the autumn. Basically all the old roses I described in Chapter 1 are shrub roses. There are also many 'new' old-fashioned shrub roses which our modern breeders have presented us with, like 'Nevada' and 'Constance Spry', which have all the beauty of the old with some modern advantages of vigour and colour.

Briefly these are the various kinds of rose readily available. How do I use them and where do I get them? Hybrid Teas and Floribundas are formal roses and best used in rose beds in separate rose gardens. The shrub roses can be used here and there about the garden as one would any other kind of shrub—perhaps given a specially prominent position if they are going to favour us with two periods of flowering. Miniature roses need special treatment, like planting them in window boxes or tubs, or using them as ribbon borders. It is obvious from their names to what use you will put ramblers and climbers and pillar roses—they are wonderful as coverer-uppers of horrors. Roses can also make good hedges.

WHERE TO BUY THEM

You can get all types of roses from the rose breeders. Every autumn come their brightly coloured catalogues, and wonderful publications they are, guaranteed to turn you into an enthusiast at once. On second thoughts, a completely confused enthusiast—so many are the kinds and shapes and colours—and, so alluring is the phraseology, you will become a penniless enthusiast, too. But here I must shout from the house-tops that rose bushes are very reasonably priced. I never cease to wonder how (when you consider what a labour-intensive industry rose growing is) the breeders manage to keep their prices so low. These days there is not only a great deal of information in the catalogues about the actual roses, but there are valuable cultural hints as well, all for the price of a stamp. Some of the catalogues are a little suspect as to the actual shade of the rose offered, however. I wince sometimes, but I am afraid one has to blame the printer rather than the grower.

One advantage of buying direct from the grower is that he has his very valuable reputation to take care of, and another is the advantageous terms one gets when purchasing a collection. The 'Fragrant Collection of Ten' or something of this kind not only gives you a cheaper price for buying ten, but also the grower will have chosen bushes with a certain uniformity for bedding out together.

The advantage of going to a garden centre is that you can buy the actual plant growing, and if you buy it in the summer you will be able to see its blooms. Of course this is rather too late to buy from a transplanting point of view: April is the very latest I would buy.

PLANTING

Season

The season for planting the bare-rooted rose bush is between October and March. In October and November the soil still has warmth from the previous summer and this will help promote new root growth before the winter. If, however, you live in an area of heavy soils and high rainfall then it is best to wait until March.

Position

Sun is important. A rose in deep shade will be unhappy and will only flourish as best it may. But perhaps you only have shade. *Rosa arvensis*—known as the Field rose—is according to the Revd Joseph Pemberton one of the most abundant of English species, and will be happy in shade; so will its progeny 'Dundee Rambler', 'Bennett's Seedling' and 'Ayrshire Splendens'. This last was called the Myrrh-scented rose and has a very individual scent. It is also Shakespeare's Musk rose:

> I know a bank where the wild thyme blows,
> Where oxslips and the nodding violet grows
> Quite over-canopied with luscious woodbine,
> With sweet musk roses and with Eglantine.

Eglantine—the Sweet briar—can perfume the air for yards around, especially after rain; the leaves give off another glorious incense. This rose, too, flourishes with me in the shade.

If you have a patch of tough grass, possibly on the edge of woodland, where there may be some shade, then the Moyesii roses will flourish in this position. They are immensely strong and vigorous.

A draughty spot is also bad. Some shelter from the prevailing wind is important. For many years I lived 12 miles (19km) from the sea in Sussex and the prevailing wind was westerly. At first my rose garden was new and exposed... and it would take time for my beech hedge to grow round it. So I lowered the rose garden by 3 feet (90cm) and had a lavender hedge round the top of the retaining wall. I then planted a beech hedge (which has the added advantage that beech retains its leaves through the winter until the wonderful pale green leaf with silver hairs forces the chestnut coloured leaf to fall in spring). Remember that a low-lying site like this needs particularly good drainage. Roses also need plenty of air, and the closeness of large trees, apart from the constant dripping, will not help them to thrive.

Soil

Roses cannot stand being water-logged, so all rose beds should have good drainage. We hear that a clay soil suits roses: it does, but it must

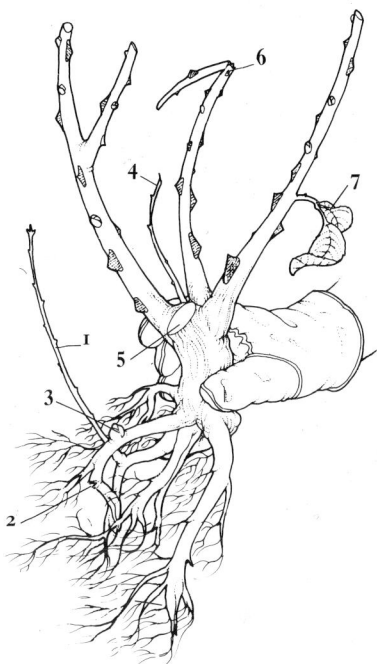

Tidying up a rose bush before planting. Indicated in the picture are: (1) a sucker from the rootstock; (2) a broken root; (3) an incipient sucker; (4) a spindly, weak shoot; (5) a 'snag', where the rootstock has been pruned; (6) a broken branch; (7) Some old leaves. All these should be pruned off before planting

23

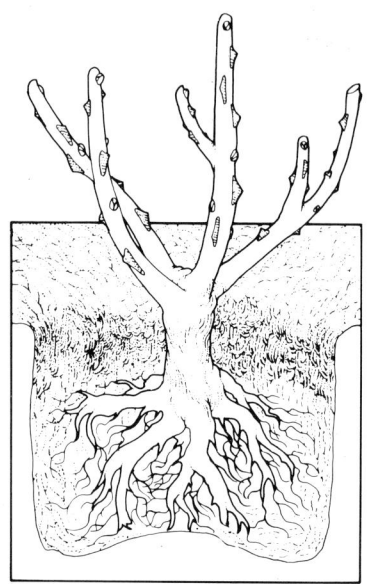

Plant the rose about 7 inches (17.5cm) deep, spreading the roots over a mound-like base in the bottom of the hole.

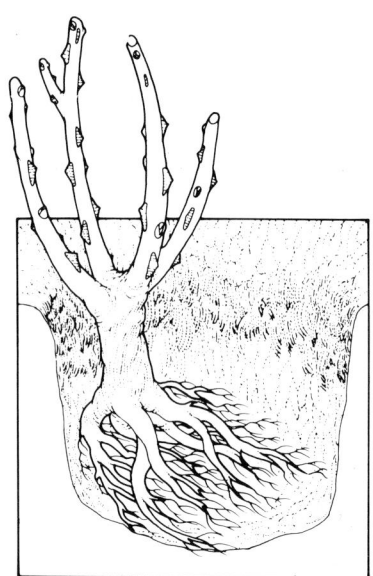

For fan-shaped roots plant with the roots facing away from the prevailing wind.

have plenty of humus to keep it open. A very heavy, wet clay will not contain enough air and an airless soil will kill; the plant suffocates. The best soil for roses is a slightly acid, medium loam, rich in humus and plant foods. Too much lime is harmful. (See what I say later on about Lime Kiln Garden, the famous rose garden in Suffolk.)

You may, thinking of the old adage that roses do best in clay, say to yourself, 'My sandy seaside soil will never nurture a rose happily.' It would nurture roses of a kind quite happily, for the Spinosissima roses come from just this kind of soil, it is their natural home. The Rugosas will flourish there too—tell me of a habitat where a Rugosa will not flourish, they are so hardy!

Pig manure is a wonderful enrichment for a light soil; it is also good for what is known as a greedy soil, providing plenty of humus as well as nutrients. Cow manure is good for a clay soil. And if you have roses in pots in a greenhouse or frame then a piece of sheep manure pressed into the soil with your thumb is most beneficial. I have seen my grandfather do this with roses and chrysanthemums, with wonderful effect!

Rose-sick soil

It is important to point out here, particularly for those of you who are about to refurbish an old garden, that roses do not like to be planted in soil where roses have grown before. There is always a possibility of the soil being rose-sick, especially if roses have been established in one place for more than ten years. The old established roses are unaffected—it is when you try to introduce new ones to an old bed that you *must* renew the soil from a part of the garden that has never grown roses before. If you are just replacing one or two dig out holes 2 feet (60cm) square and 2 feet (60cm) deep and renew, digging plenty of organic matter into the new soil. Remember that peat is only a soil 'conditioner': it does not feed as compost and well-decayed manure will do.

Planting a bare-rooted rose

The weather will play you awful tricks when your roses arrive. You should never plant in water-logged soil, or snow, or frost, so you may have to delay until the weather relents. If it is frosty store the package, unopened, in an unheated garage or shed; the roses will last indefinitely as long as the weather remains cold. If the temperature rises open the package, pour some water on the plants, wrap the roots in polythene, and store, again in an unheated garage or shed, out of draughts and out of the sun. Examine the plants daily and damp them when necessary. Or you could heel them in, in a shallow trench in the garden, covering the roots with some dry soil from the frames or the greenhouse. Never leave a pile of roses with their roots exposed to wind or sun, even for half an hour. Take the one you are about to plant and put a damp sack over the other roots. Transplanting even a dormant shrub is giving the poor thing some kind of shock, so every bit of cossetting will help. Explain to it what you are up to—so long as nobody is about!

When you unpack your rose take the secateurs and cut off any leaves, buds or heps present. Cut off any damaged and puny branches. If the roots appear dry plunge in a bucket of water for an hour or so. Also, if any roots appear damaged cut them off, and shorten any over-long root.

Having dug compost and well-rotted manure (not poultry manure as it is too strong) into the soil and added half a handful of sterilized bonemeal, you make each hole 2 feet (60cm) wide and 7 inches (17.5cm) deep—this should be deep enough, as roses like to have their roots sitting horizontally on the bottom of the hole. Spread all the roots like the spokes of an umbrella over a mound-like base to the hole. Ideally the bud union should be just at ground level—do make sure it isn't above the ground. Now sprinkle round some peat or fine soil, or better still some grow-bag material (new, not exhausted) to encourage the young roots to explore. Firm down with some more of your planting mixture, then fill up with soil. All of this you firm down, but do not jump about on the soil you have replaced as some enthusiasts do—one must not impact the soil, or damage the roots. Come back and firm later, in case the wind has rocked your plant. Sometimes a rose arrives with all its roots pointing one way. If so, make a fan-shaped hole and plant, keeping the roots well parted but pointing in the same direction. Make sure you plant against the prevailing wind so the shrub is well anchored.

If you are planting a new rose bed it is best to use bamboo canes to mark out exactly where you want your bushes to be. This will ensure an even spacing.

Planting container-grown roses

With container-grown roses you make your hole of suitable depth to house the soil of the container and leave a space of 6 inches (15cm) or so around and under the container. This is to be filled up with the planting mixture, be it grow-bag or whatever, as more than likely the container-grown rose will be in a peaty compost and the roots will very much dislike attacking the hard texture of ordinary garden soil and will ball up and never explore out into the rose bed's permanent soil. If you transplant in the summer remember that frequent watering is imperative, especially of all the foliage in the evening.

FEEDING

Your roses are the healthiest you can buy, you have transplanted them as carefully as possible in exactly the right place. Your job now? To keep them healthy and to enjoy their generosity of bloom.

All living things, be they human, animal or vegetable, need the right food, in the right quantities, at the right time, so that they can grow to maturity and remain healthy. The Hon. Treasurer of the Royal National Rose Society in 1976, Mr E. V. Elwes (a distinguished chemist), writing in the *Rose Annual* of that year, said: 'Out of a mere handful of common chemical elements—chiefly carbon, oxygen, nitrogen and hydrogen with lesser amounts of phosphorus, magnesium, potassium, iron, silicon, aluminium, manganese and boron, a rose tree can produce a spectrum of pigments in both leaves and petals to give us the thousands of variations that we see and enjoy in the roses in our gardens.'

First and foremost your soil must have a good physical structure

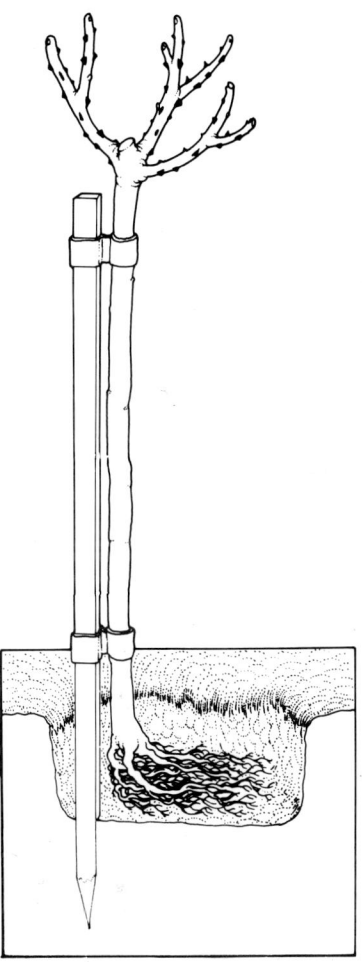

When planting a standard, put the stake in first to avoid damage to the roots. Make sure the top of the stake is below the head of the standard, otherwise some of the stems are sure to get rubbed. Tie firmly to the stake, and press roots well in, with the ends pointing away from the prevailing wind.

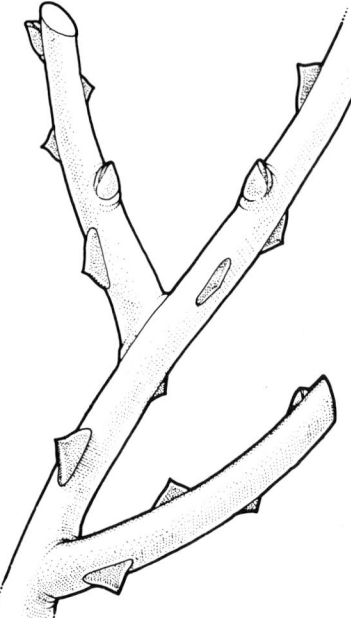

When pruning, make a clean cut above an outward-facing bud. Slant the cut so that water rolls off.

containing plenty of humus, so that whatever feed you give will get to those tiny, venturing roots when it rains. 'Every good gardener should have a keen sense of humus.' The soil should contain farmyard manure, chopped turf, peat and compost. This way it will remain 'open'. What I do is this—and it is the pessimist's use of belt and braces! Every year I get from a local farmer several loads of farmyard manure, horse manure too if I can. This I compost with grass cuttings and weeds so that it heats up to such an extent that all seeds are destroyed (I hope—they never are completely). I use it as a liberal mulch in March. Then in case this lovely rich mixture—looking like a friable Xmas pudding by the time I use it—has not got every element the roses need, according to Mr Elwes, I add Rose Plus, or some similar special rose fertilizer, once the weather and a bit of hoeing have settled the compost mixture into a friable tilth (I knew this term would creep into the book sooner or later—it always does. . .). The birds, damn them, also help with this, by showering the stuff all over the paths—dwarf edgings of box, lavender, pinks or, believe it or not, chives will not prevent this. (I am going to digress again here: 'Chives?' you say. 'Yes,' I reply, 'The members of the onion family—garlic is a favourite—when planted amongst roses will keep away green fly and all sorts of nastiness!') Use about a heaped tablespoonful of fertilizer around each tree—and this you can repeat, as I do, after the first flush of flowering to build up the strength of your plants to ensure a good second crop of blooms in August and September.

There is an important rider here: do not use rose fertilizer towards the end of the season, as the potash will stimulate new growth at the wrong time. Frost will damage the new growth before it has time to harden and disease spores, ever at the ready it seems to me, will dash in and wreak havoc.

Using both natural and synthetic foods you can argue with faddists on either side of the fence. But if I had to choose between the two I would choose the natural one every time.

Some rose growers use a sprinkling of bonemeal in the winter. It

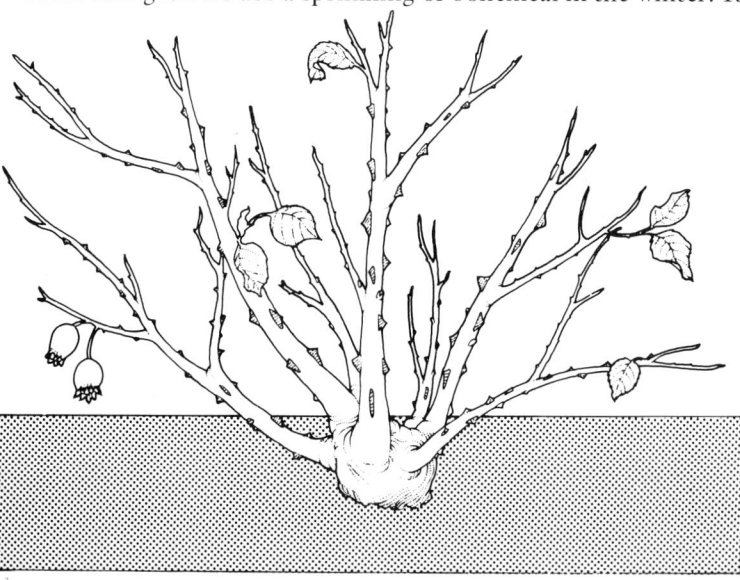

A mature Hybrid Tea rose before pruning.

is slow-acting and can only do good. Use only the sterilized kind please, for fear of anthrax—a dread and often fatal disease contracted from decomposing bones in the soil. Fish meal is advocated by some but I cannot bear the pong! Dried blood I eschew for the same reason.

Foliar feeding—spraying the leaves with a special fertilizer added to water—I do not practise. Many do it at the same time as spraying against disease, using the same mixture. This you do in the summer.

A pinch or two of Epsom Salts is said to help the foliage. It's never helped mine! Also, some people say that you should not over-feed newly planted trees. After all one does not give a baby caviar!

PRUNING

Pruning is our next controversial step. To prune is not controversial: all roses must be pruned as they flower on new wood. I must make a correction here: some shrub roses do not need annual pruning, but Hybrid Teas and Floribundas do. The controversy always rages about whether to prune in the autumn or the spring. Being an equable chap I do both! If a bush has grown very large and especially high in the summer then I do not want it to rock and tear itself to pieces in every winter gale, so I take about a third of it away. Then, come the Spring—and hopefully before the end of March—I prune properly.

How does one prune properly? It comes instinctively to me now, so I must think hard and give you advice step by step.

Through the year parts of your tree will die. Some will have become diseased, some damaged by storms or animals. Prune all the dead wood out—it will usually be a different brown colour from the normal green of the bush. When you cut the wood should show white: this means you have cut back to healthy wood. Should it show brown cut lower still into the good wood until the cut shows white. Cut diagonally (so that rain will run off the sloping cut and not linger to rot the wood) above an outward pointing bud. Make sure you cut near the bud, and the cut must be clean (not jagged). Never leave

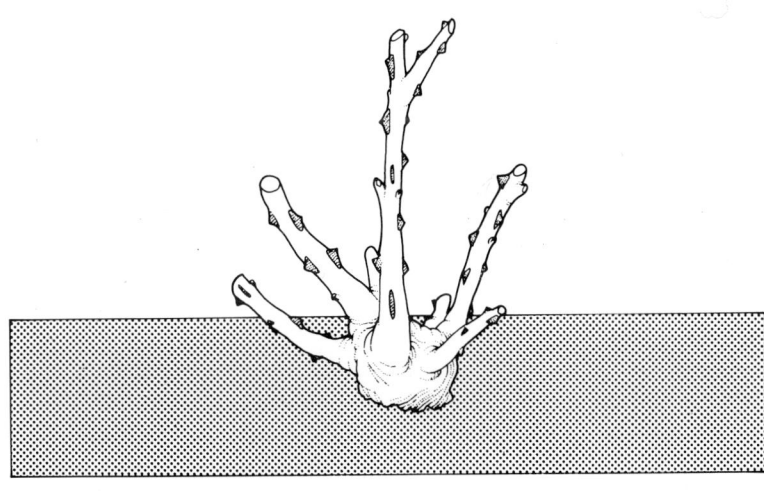

The same Hybrid Tea rose after pruning.

No meaner hand may discipline
the shoots,
None but his steel approach
them. What is weak,
Distempered, or has lost
prolific powers,
Impaired by age, his
unrelenting hand
Dooms to the knife; nor does
he spare the soft
And succulent, that feeds its
giant growth,
But barren, at the expense of
neighbouring twigs
Less ostentatious, and yet
studded thick
With hopeful gems. The rest,
no portion left
That may disgrace his art, or
disappoint
Large expectation, he disposes
neat
At measured distances, that air
and sun
Admitted freely may afford
their aid,
And ventilate and warm the
swelling buds.
WILLIAM COWPER, 1731–1800

prunings about on the ground: if you do it will encourage disease. Then remove all the thin 'wappetty' stems and any branches which are rubbing against each other: where the rubbing takes place disease can get in under the bruised skin. Ideally, if you cut to an outward-facing bud each time, when the summer comes the whole bush will be growing outwards and the inside of the bush will be light and airy. Cut out any soft wood (usually reddish) which the sun of last summer did not ripen. The rest of the bush is now healthy but unpruned. Hard pruning is usually done on newly planted roses to stimulate root growth, and for exhibition blooms. You cut back to three or four buds, leaving the bush 5 inches (12.5cm) high.

After the first year cut back the main stems of Hybrid Teas to half the length. The harder you prune the longer from that date it will take for your bushes to flower. Mindful of this, if you prune half your roses a bit harder than the other half then you will have a longer season of bloom, and by the time the harder pruned bushes have finished blooming the more lightly pruned ones will be offering a second flowering. Floribundas should never be pruned as hard as Hybrid Teas, about half as much. And don't prune standards too hard: the head of a bush should be shaped like a wine glass, with open space in the centre for light and growth.

With ramblers cut out the branches which have flowered and tie in the new growth in the autumn. Climbing roses you do not prune at all—just cut out the dead wood, dead tips usually, and if the bush gets very overcrowded after a few years thin out to improve the shape of the tree and to encourage growth further down. Species roses and shrub roses I hardly prune at all.

You prune a little by judicious dead-heading. It will waste the energy of your rose to allow the dead heads to form heps and inhibit the formation of new buds. Do not just cut off the flower at the top of the stem but cut down to the second or third leaf. When cutting blooms for the house do not take too long a stem from any bush, and certainly not several long stems from one bush.

A sucker is a growth from the stock on to which your rose has been budded. If you let it grow, as the root stock or briar is stronger than the variety budded on to it, it will eventually take over the whole bush and you will have a Rugosa or a wild rose instead of a Hybrid Tea or Floribunda. So it is necessary to remove the sucker (which is usually growing from the root) from below the surface of the soil. It is no good just pruning it off at soil level.

DISEASES

Having fed and pruned and planted with care all you should now look forward to are the blossoms. Please do not over-lime, and take care not to overcrowd or to over-prune year after year. Unfortunately, no matter how careful you are, and no matter how healthy and how strong they are, some bushes will be attacked by rose diseases.

Blackspot is possibly the worst and most prevalent of the diseases—though when Carlyle wrote, 'Always there is a black spot in our sunshine', he certainly did not have rose disease in mind! The maddening thing is the clearer your air is, the more likelihood there is of your roses suffering. The spores flourish by the sea and in the open country. The black spots, with their yellow fringes, are also encouraged by lack of potash in the soil, and the disease is worse in a wet, hot, humid summer.

Blackspot spreads rapidly, causing the leaves to fall. It will often start in June and by the end of August and September will completely de-foliate a bush. Even shoots will die back from it. Always gather and destroy the leaves left on the ground. It is often thought that the spores of the disease come from the ground. Spray tree and surrounding soil with Benlate and follow up with another spray a week later.

I was once being shown round Great Dixter Gardens by that admired and learned gardener Christopher Lloyd. 'How often do you spray against blackspot?' I asked as I admired the clean rose leaves.

'Never,' he said.

'What is so different with you?' I said, 'with my living a few miles away and with my bushes so heavily attacked?'

'I do not let it begin,' he said, and then explained that he mulched his roses with grass mowings about 3 inches (7.5cm) deep, right through the summer. After about three years the blackspot had disappeared, never to return. I then used his method—untidy though it was with the birds scratching it out on to the paths—and after two years or so I no longer needed to spray. One year, so exasperated was I with the untidiness of the rose garden, I gave orders for no more mulching: the next year the blackspot was back. Why not do a first spraying and then use a mulch of peat on a damp day and see what happens? This is something I mean to do one summer. Or use the ICI composted bark—this should make a good layer, though on a wet day it does smell strongly of coniferous wood.

Mildew is perhaps the next worst scourge, disfiguring the leaves. It also attacks the dark red roses with greater ferocity. Use Toprose Mildew Spray once a week for two months—and later in the season vary it with some other proprietary named remedy. Rust is not common but it is fatal. Orange swellings on the leaves herald this scourge; they turn black in August. The remedy here is to spray with Plantvax. All this spraying is expensive and boring, though the introduction of the systemic fungicide has made life much easier. What happens here, as with the systemic insecticide, is that the plant absorbs the chemical into its sap stream and the disease or insect then absorbs the poison and gives in. But trouble will come if you only use one particular brand: the enemy gets resistant to it, so you want to change your chemical every year or so and laugh all the way to the chemist. Then the chemist can laugh all the way to the bank.

Leafcutter bee, leaf miner, caterpillars from various moths (Lackey, Winter, Vapourer, Yellow-tail and Buff-tip), red spider mite, rose slugworm, leaf-hoppers, capsid bugs, tortrix moth maggot, chafer beetle, leaf-rolling sawfly (sounds like a DIY fanatic from insect land!) and greenfly—all will try to assail your bushes at some time or other and all will succumb to systemic insecticide. There is a new killer on the market which rejoices in the poetic name of Tumble-bug!

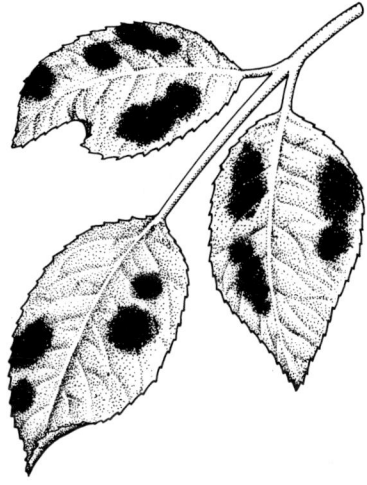

Blackspot shows like an ink blotch with a fringe of yellow. This spreads and the leaves frequently drop off.

So what have we to aim for? Who better than J. L. Harkness, rose nurseryman, breeder and judge. He calls these 'three times three', the recipe for a rose:
The Plant: Vigour, Habit, Health
The Flower: Form, Colour, Continuity (the number of flowers over a season)
The Variety: Fragrance, Effect, Novelty

3

Climbing & Rambler Roses ~ and roses for hedges

It was Gertrude Jekyll, that great Victorian gardener who resisted the fashion of regimented flowers, who brought the ramblers and the climbing roses back into favour. She needed the Sleeping Beauty look of abandoned luxuriance, and here to give it were festoons of carefree blossom. After all the native Dog rose is a rambler, and much of its beauty lies in the way a long trailing branch of bloom will suddenly throw itself over the hedge to greet us with its wild natural grace.

Roses are not climbers in the sense that ivy is, with its suckers which hold it to a tree or wall, or clematis, with its tendrils which search out for and hold on to a support. Roses will hang down the sides of cliffs or mountains, or once up a tree will cascade down from it like an exotic waterfall. The ramblers have softer, more whip-like stems and are easier to train; they don't even mind being shown round corners! The climbers are more like the sport of Hybrid Teas and Floribundas, which in many instances they are. All have to be tied into supports, against trellis, walls, pergolas and arches, over gazebos and summerhouses, and, of course, up and through trees and against the house.

When training—persuading is a better word—the tender-soft new shoots of the rambler great care must be used, not only with the soft tips of the trailing branches but at the place where they join the main stem. You may think you have persuaded the branch into exactly the right position when it gives way at the joint—and you may have to wait a whole season to get another branch in the right spot. Finding shoots for the lower areas is often the difficulty.

Some gardeners do not like the formality of the Hybrid Tea bush

---

Right: 'Lawrence Johnston' growing on a pillar at Bone Hill. It is named after the creator of Hidcote, that great Cotswold garden.

'Paul's Himalayan Musk'
cascading over the trees in the
orchard at Lime Kiln Garden.
Mountainous indeed!
And steeped in fragrance.

or the sort of rose gardens with separate rose beds which their form dictates, yet they yearn for the perfect formal shape and scent of the Hybrid Tea bloom. A climbing rose which is a sport of the Hybrid Tea is their heaven-sent answer. Very roughly, the rambler rose is the wild or species rose, usually and sadly with only one flowering period as in the wild, and the climbers are the hybrids, mostly with large flowers and many of them repeat flowering.

Pillar roses are usually the sports of Hybrid Teas or new varieties grown from seed. They reach perhaps 8 or 9 feet (2.4–2.7m) in height and are best as their name describes them, usually tied to the pillar of an arch or pergola, or on to a free-standing tripod of poles or trellis.

Most books concentrate on the actual climbers and ramblers to grow. I shall mention my favourites and why they are my favourites as we go along, and later in the book we shall meet personally and discuss many roses as they enchant us in the various gardens we visit and photograph—and, as the gardens I have chosen are famous and fairly accessible, you may be able to go and make their acquaintance for yourselves before choosing them. What I want to concentrate on here is how you treat them once you have got them home.

Roses in trees

So many people in my phone-ins on Capital Radio tell me they have a large tree and do not know what to do with it or how to treat it. I make a plea to save the tree's life first of all. I point out that with one of those horrid-sounding electric saws you can fell a tree in half an

A Sport
A rose tree will be growing quite happily in a garden for perhaps five years when suddenly capricious Mother Nature, for no apparent reason, will make a new branch grow and produce a completely different flower, either in colour or form. This is known as a sport.

This house is transformed by
the rose ('Pink Perpêtue')
growing all over its walls.
Note the empty
square of trellis to the left.

hour which has taken a century to grow. Once felled it cannot be
replaced in a lifetime. Think twice, think many times, before you
remove one. 'Underneath it', I advise, 'there are many plants which
are happy in dry shade.' Well, not many, but I make it sound quite a
lot. And then I make a big thing of how you can plant a quick-
growing rambler which in a couple of years will throw a cascade of
blossom, scented and coloured, through and down from the tallest
tree. Or perhaps two ramblers of contrasting form and colour.

Exuberant ramblers like *R. filipes* 'Kiftsgate', *R. longicuspis* and
R. rubus, when planted next to the tree they will eventually climb,
cover and hang down gloriously from, need special thought when
planting. You must put the roots well away from the tree, so that the
plant can get light and rain, then train the first shoots into the host's
branches above. It will ease matters if you can plant the rose on the
windward side of the tree: the prevailing wind will then take the
trailing shoots into the tree instead of away from it.

Roses on the walls of your house
If your garden is small there may not be room for the exuberance of
the rambler, and upwards may be the only way you can expand
without annoying your neighbours or the local surveyor. Clothe
your house with roses. Be careful here to give proper regard to the
actual colour of your house walls. If they are painted white, or
wedgewood green (a perfect foil for a pink or dark red rose), then all
is well—but a pale pink washed house must be dealt with carefully,
for a pale pink rose might be 'lost' against it and a rusty pink might

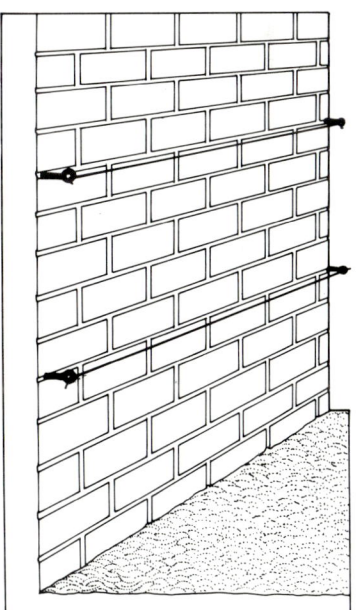

Vine-eyes and wire for training
a climbing or rambler rose
against a house wall.

33

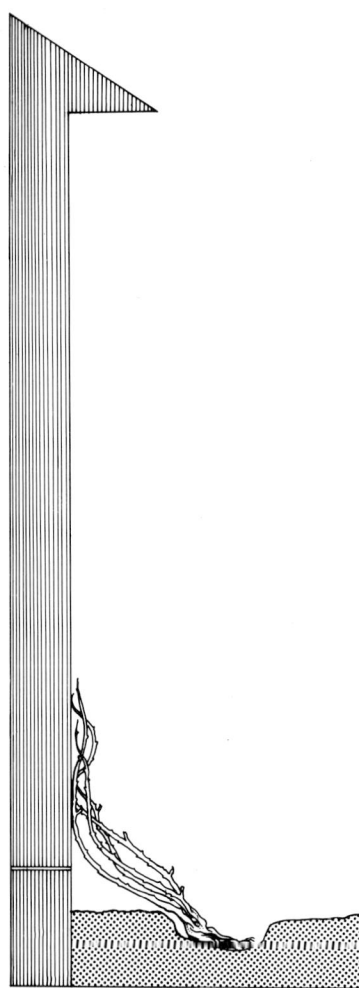

Plant a good 18 inches (45cm) away from the wall of the house so that the roots have room and can get moisture away from the eaves. Be sure the soil level is below the damp-course.

clash. Yellow would be your best bet here. Blue walls I would not permit you to have anyway. A red brick wall needs care: if it is old and weathered and mature, your rose will enhance and caress it no matter what its colour, but if it is new and bright be careful to choose some soft colours to help it. Yellow brick needs strong glossy foliage, and perhaps pink and red roses. If your house is built of Cotswold stone, or Bath stone, or Portland stone, or any other natural stone—Kentish ragstone is my favourite—then you are a lucky gardener indeed. Any colour rose will enhance the beauty and warmth of these.

Think, too, of which way your walls face. A south-facing wall holds so much warmth that here is the best home for the more tender roses. You may also find that a climbing rose grown against a house will bloom more generously around the top windows; try and encourage the lower growth to sprout and flower but, if necessary, fill this space in with a tall-growing shrub rose or Floribunda or pillar rose to make sure there is not a single foot of space wasted. 'Iceberg' we know as a lovely climber—but if she is not giving enough bloom in her nether regions, plant in front some bushes of Floribunda-type 'Iceberg' to make sure all is covered.

When planting your rose near a house wall make sure you plant below the damp course and do please remember that the eaves of a house make the ground near to it very dry. Plant at least 18 inches (45cm) away from the house, add lots of humus to the soil to contain what moisture there will be, and tie a knot in your handkerchief to remind you to water well in a dry spell.

There are two ways to attach your rose to the house. Either tie it in to panels of wooden trellis attached to the house, or use wire and 'vine-eyes'. This to my mind is the most effective, most permanent way, and it leads to a greater uniformity of coverage because you do the whole side of the house at one go and then tie your rose on to the wires as it grows. If you are building a new house it is best to have the vine-eyes built into it at regular intervals: otherwise you must first drill your hole and insert the vine-eye and then point with mortar. Vine-eyes, as the name suggests, were invented to train vines on greenhouse walls, and they are really a pointed staple about 3 inches (7.5cm) long with a hole at one end through which you thread a thick wire. At intervals of 2 feet (60cm) up the wall and about 6 feet (1.8m) along the wall these will give you the necessary support.

Roses on fences

Suburban gardens are cursed with fences. They make a long monotonous plane of usually creosoted wood. (Do not use creosote for your fences—it exudes fumes which are sometimes fatal to plants. The only use I have for creosote in my garden is to dip the ends of posts into before putting them in the ground.) Fences make perfect supports for roses to grow against. Either tie them to the fence or nail panels of Netlon or similar netting or panels of wooden trellis to the fence. Make sure the actual posts holding it up are all good and solid and properly in the ground, as your roses will give added weight to the fence. Panels of trellis on top of it will help your privacy and, being open woodwork, will give helpful air and room to

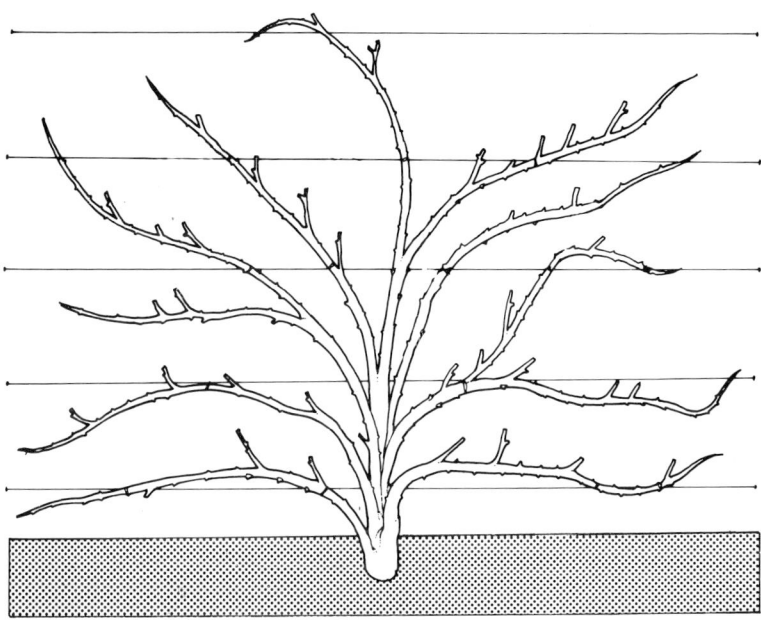

Training a climbing rose on a
wall. Make sure the
shoots do not overlap each
other, otherwise they will
rub, causing damage
and encouraging disease.

the growing rose. One must remember that a solid fence or wall does mean that a rose can only get sun and light from one side.

Split chestnut paling makes a long-lasting, open fence, very suitable for supporting climbing and rambler roses. Look at the picture opposite of a fence designed by me for one of my Chelsea gardens: it shows panels of wood with a Chinese Chippendale idiom supported by stone pillars. Roses over these fences would be delightful. Posts and rails of white wood boarding (an American inspiration) also make good fences for roses.

Pergolas, arches and porches

Pergolas are covered walks consisting of pillars on either side of wood, stone or brick, with wooden cross-beams above supported by the pillars. The pillars provide supports for the roses, which then fill in the roof as it were with stems and flowers. A pergola is really a rose arbour extending open-ended to become a covered walk. It is an enchanting way to exploit and show off climbing and rambler roses.

It is not necessary to have a large garden to have a pergola. Imagine one which has the side of your house for one side and pillars for the other, with cross-beams and roses filling in the roof. This makes a kind of pergola terrace for the house, and as you look out of the french windows you will see the rest of the garden as a picture, or series of pictures, framed by rose-covered pillars. You will need a path beneath your pergola—perhaps York stone paving slabs, or simulated York paving made by Atlas, Mucklow or Haddonstone—there are many first-class manufacturers.

Arches placed at strategic points in the garden, made of larch poles, trellis or wire, are another effective way of displaying roses. Porches over the house door can also be made of similar materials and, according to the character of the house, can be very effective. Guard against the desire to put a rural, rustic archway over the door of a modern concrete house. They spoil each other.

This Chinese Chippendale
fence I designed for one of my
Chelsea gardens would
be perfect for
growing roses against.

The gazebo I designed for the Capital Radio garden at the 1979 Chelsea Flower Show.

Summerhouses and gazebos

Many a romance has been started on a garden seat under a rose-covered arch or arbour. Extending the idiom we come to the summerhouse or gazebo. In a large garden a summerhouse is not only useful as a focal point, or as a genuine shelter if it is some distance from the house, but it is often an excellent store for the mower, the tennis posts and net, and the croquet hoops! (No sir, not big enough for the polo ponies!) To marry the building in with the scene cover it with roses.

There is then the garden gazebo. The dictionary defines a gazebo as 'a structure where a view may be had', but it is really there for decoration and might be called a folly! In short, it is a building from a dream, made solely for your delight and caparisoned with roses. Gazebos may be built of brick or stone to resemble temples or colombariums, in which case they are major edifices and expensive, or they can be airy-fairy constructions of white painted trellis and less costly. I designed one for my garden at Chelsea one year, and had so many enquiries about it that it is now manufactured as a regular line, but it would be even more engaging if it were a riot of roses.

Trellis

Which brings me quite naturally to trellis. Trellis, or trelliage as it should be called, is made of wooden lattice, either in squares or diamond shapes (the extended kind). It can be used with trellis pillars in panels, as it was by the French in the days of the Empire, and by the English in Victorian times, and by me and some other garden designers today.

Trellis panels are useful as they will hide anything. They make a very good boundary. Trellis pillars connected by ropes for the roses to garland, as used in Queen Mary's Rose Garden at Regents Park, are another wonderful way of displaying the climbing and rambler rose. Trellis can be used as panels on walls and fencing; properly framed it can be used as gates. It is quite strong and sturdy yet it is at the same time airy, illusory and insubstantial-looking—just right for supporting so ethereal a conceit as garlands of coloured, scented blossoms.

There are quite attractive pierced concrete walls which make an effective support for roses; you can get particulars from the Cement Association. If your garden is exposed to all winds, use the blocks to make a large circle with a fair-sized opening—a bit like a horseshoe—and up to 7 feet (2.1m) high. Inside the circle make a border a foot (30cm) wide for your climbing roses, then a path and then a circular centre bed for Floribundas or Hybrid Teas, with perhaps a weeping standard in the middle.

Growing clematis with rambler roses

Shall we suppose that the once-flowering climber or rambler (usually it is the rambler) poses a problem because of its short flowering period. If it does we have a wonderful ally and cure in the clematis. It is important to choose the gentle kind not, I beg of you, a *Clematis montana*, which is a vigorous species and would overwhelm your rose. You could start with *C. cirrhosa balearica*, which has fern-like leaves, bronze in winter, and yellow flowers like creamy hellebores; it flowers in winter or early spring, thus extending your season. In the autumn *C. tangutica* hangs yellow lanterns followed by silky seed heads. Then there are the big-flowered clematis—so richly endowed with various blues. These are the Clematis Jackmannii. These normally flower in late summer on the current year's shoots. The following are useful ones to have amongst roses: *C. ×Jackmannii superba*—with large, rich purple flowers from July to September; 'Mme Edouard André', with rich crimson flowers with yellow stamens, free-flowering from June to August; and 'Mrs Cholmondeley', with large, pale blue flowers from May to August—put her with a pale pink rose and they will flower together.

C. patens 'Vyvyan Pennell' has large, deep violet-blue flowers suffused with purple and carmine in the centre; it has double flowers from May to July, and then flowers again in the autumn, this time producing single blooms. It is almost as lovely as a rose! The crimson 'Gravetye Beauty' and the pink 'Duchess of Albany' are less vigorous than the other clematis I have mentioned, and for the timorous might be the ones to start with. If you work out the flowering of your rose and your clematis so that one is out when the

'Seagull' growing magnificently on a pergola at Bone Hill, the Royal National Rose Society garden at St Albans. This is a very vigorous rambler.

other is not, then colour combinations will be of no consequence.

It is best not to plant the rose and the clematis at the same time. Give the rose a couple of years' start, then plant the clematis near it so that the rose will shade its roots. In its natural habitat the clematis is a forest climber, so it likes to have its roots in the shade and then to climb upwards so that its flowers are in the sun. If we only knew, of all plants, where they came from and how they grew in the wild, then we could meet them halfway with the conditions we give them and have much happier plants and more successful gardens.

ROSES FOR HEDGES

Roses make perfect hedges for the garden, be they used for boundaries or for 'inside' hedges to cut up a large garden into small 'rooms'. A hedge all of one variety and blooming magnificently would be too much, too overwhelming for all your other flowers and too drab when the flowering season was over. The most effective hedge will surely consist of short runs of different species, and different varieties of each species. Some hedges can be 10 feet (3m) tall, to hide your garden from the outside world, while others could be 4 feet (1.2m), perhaps more, to form pleasant shelter for rose beds within each 'room'.

Your rose hedges will need other hedges and shrubs of different plants to complement them and to give them atmosphere and a sense of period. Yew will do this. I visualize a hedge of perhaps 20 feet (6m) or so then a yew pillar of topiary acting as a finial, then perhaps an opening for a gate followed by another pillar of yew and then another run of rose hedge.

For an outside boundary one needs to find a rose sufficiently thick and thorny to dismay cattle and/or small boys; Sweet briar would do this. The Penzance briars—close relatives with larger flowers—would be equally effective. 'Albertine' is a very dense, robust rose—and although its magnificent flowering season is short the foliage is very attractive and in milder areas evergreen. Also pale salmon pink, fading to white, with a repeat performance that 'Albertine' never

gives, is the Hybrid Musk rose 'Penelope'. Another is 'Buff Beauty', with its apricot-beige colouring.

The Rugosa roses can be used for hedges. 'Sarah Van Fleet' is fragrant pink with a touch of lilac and always in bloom and so is 'Roseraie de l'Hay', with flat semi-double blooms of rich crimson-purple (the colour of a retired admiral's nose who is addicted to port!). Mine are gloriously scented, and although they are never covered in bloom there are always some flowers about. It might be a nice idea to make a hedge of alternate shrubs—leave a good 3 feet (90cm) for each to spread and they will grow to 4 or 5 feet (1.2–1.5m) tall. Do not prune much—just keep the shrubs from straying! 'Scabrosa' has the largest blooms of all, a pinky mauve. The advantage of the Rugosas is that they are always disease-free, and if they sucker it will be from their own roots, which will help to make the hedge thicker and more useful.

'Queen Elizabeth' is a tall-growing Floribunda. It will bloom all summer through and grow to 15 feet (4.5m) or so if allowed. The only trouble with this rose when used as a hedge is that nearly all the blooms will appear at the top if you do not prune some of the branches. There are other tall Floribundas, too, like 'Dorothy Wheatcroft', and 'Peace', so gloriously robust, which will grow to 5 feet (1.5m) (do not be tempted to use the climbing 'Peace' as it is very shy of flowering). If you use these vigorous Floribundas and Hybrid Teas as a hedge you will need to plant closely together and prune at about 2 feet (60cm).

You could afford to have as long a run as you like of *R. primula*—the Incense rose (with its fabulous aroma)—or 'Canary Bird', with their primrose-like blooms, because they will flower earlier in the season than your other roses—in April in Sussex with me. For the rest of the year the soft fernlike foliage will make an excellent foil for other blooms, and the dark, claret-coloured stems are most amenable to training.

There is a modern shrub rose, 'Frühlingsgold', which is a cross between a Hybrid Tea and the Burnet or Scots briar. It has huge arching branches and large, creamy yellow, semi-double flowers in clusters; it will grow 7 feet (2.1m) wide and 7 feet (2.1m) high, and it is fragrant. This will make a good hedge, but it will need time to fill the spaces between the plants after you first put them in. The Sweet briar is fast-growing and cheap, so it is a good practical idea to fill in with perhaps two Sweet briars in between each of your 'Frühlingsgolds' and, as these develop and grow over three or four years, remove the Sweet briars one by one.

If you have somewhere in the garden where you want a hedge to provide strong autumn colour then the American rose *R. virginiana* is a late-flowering, spreading shrub with glossy leaves, pink scented flowers and the most spectacular orange autumnal foliage interspersed with red heps.

When planting your rose hedge cultivate the site well, giving it plenty of humus and other food—the hedge will be there a long time. Remember, it will not be evergreen and you will not be able to use shears and prune it into a neat, squared off outline. But no other shrub used as a hedge will give you such a long period of bloom.

4

Roses for Ground Cover~ and ground cover for roses

The cost of labour prevents many a gardening enthusiast from expanding, and the amount of labour required to run a successful garden becomes daunting as one gets older , so we crafty gardeners are constantly finding easier ways to do things, easier, more vigorous plants and new ways of using chemicals and sprays. Now I am an enthusiastic *natural* gardener and do not like the use of weed-killers (though I do confess to the use of one containing simazine for paths strictly one application a year, with all dogs and children hidden in the house, gas-masks given to the goldfish, all empty and half-empty cartons destroyed, and all watering cans washed out thoroughly—and believe it or not I also wash my shoes after using it). But it does save endless hours of weeding paths, and the time thus saved I can spend in the garden doing more useful things like planting roses in the borders to act as ground cover to suppress weeds.

ROSES FOR GROUND COVER

There are some roses of sufficiently lax growth, which sprawl, too short for training upwards but too long for shrubs: these are the ones for us to peg down, which will on their own become carpeters, often creating dense, hummocky ground cover. Sam McGredy, in his latest book *Look to the Rose* (Collins, 1982), says: '"Snow Carpet" is the first step on the way to something new in roses . . . Niels Poulsen proved it is a real ground cover rose. He walked all over his plants last year, while I was with him in Denmark. The next day there was no trace of his rough treatment.' It is tiny with small, double, creamy white flowers. It

---

Right: Hedge of 'Roseraie de l'Hay' under-planted with *Geranium* 'Johnson's Blue' at Bone Hill, the RNRS garden near St Albans.

'Max Graf' is a vigorous trailing shrub, excellent for ground cover.

looks lovely to me. 'Peek-a-Boo' is a new apricot-orange, short, bushy Floribunda from Dicksons. *R. nitida* comes from North America and has small shining leaves, with small single pink flowers in June and July; it forms a low spreading plant 18 inches (45cm) high and 2 feet (60cm) wide. Very pale pink, almost white, is 'Nozomi', while 'Raubritter' has a double pink tiny cabbage-like flower—these two are both featured at Bone Hill, the RNRS grounds near St Albans. 'Max Graf' looks very like a darker pink version of our Dog rose—it's a good example of the rooting rambler, rooting when the canes touch the soil. 'Temple Bells' is another rooting and spreading rose, excellent for awkward areas like banks. It has small, single, white, rather battered-looking blooms. The Elizabethan Gillyflower rose, a dwarf with bottle-green foliage, might be considered for ground cover, but its existence seems a little doubtful. Mrs Nancy Lindsay sent a few cuttings to Vita Sackville-West, saying that the blooms of a Tudor rose as depicted were not stylized versions but exact copies of this little rose's double ruby-red formal flowers. (This piece of interesting gardening gossip I purloined from *Down to Earth Women*, a delightful book on women gardeners by Dawn MacLeod (Blackwood, 1982).)

There is a green rose suitable for ground cover—*R. chinensis* 'Viridiflora'. Hilliers call it 'a curious small shrub with double flowers consisting of numerous crowded, greenish petal-like scales'. I bet the flower arrangers go mad about this! This does not spread but you could grow it very closely.

Other good ground cover roses are the Harkness roses 'Fairy Changeling' (variable shades of rose pink); 'Fairy Crystal'; 'Fairy Damsel' (deep ox-blood red), which is definitely prostrate and will spread sideways to cover 3–4 feet (90–120cm) of ground with its dark shiny foliage; 'Fairyland', a double white tinged with pinky mauve; and 'Fairy Prince', which is geranium-lake in colour. Like 'Fairyland', this forms a hummock of dainty foliage decorated all over with fragrant rosettes. Though only 2½ feet (75cm) high it can be 5–6 feet (1.5–1.8m) wide, so plant them at least 4 feet (1.2m) apart.

One could use 'Ballerina', too, as a ground cover rose, as it spreads densely. It is a modern shrub rose with single pink blooms with a white centre; it spreads to 4 feet by 4 feet (1.2 × 1.2m).

The Polypompon rose 'Gruss an Aachen' grows in bushes 2 feet (60cm) square, so if you bedded an area with it its good glossy foliage would suppress weeds. It has flesh-pink flowers, double and slightly fragrant, which fade to cream, and the joyous habit of almost continuous flowering. It would also make a good low hedge.

So you see it needs many visits to gardens and garden centres before you decide exactly how and where you will use roses for ground cover. Many can be used with artistic ingenuity which at first sight do not seem exactly right. Be mindful of their habit and size, and of the exact nature of the corner you need to fill, and do not be guided by the purist—try things out. Another major advantage roses have over so many other shrubs is that they will move quite happily so long as you use care and do so at the dormant season.

The modern shrub rose 'Ballerina' can also be used for ground cover, as it spreads densely.

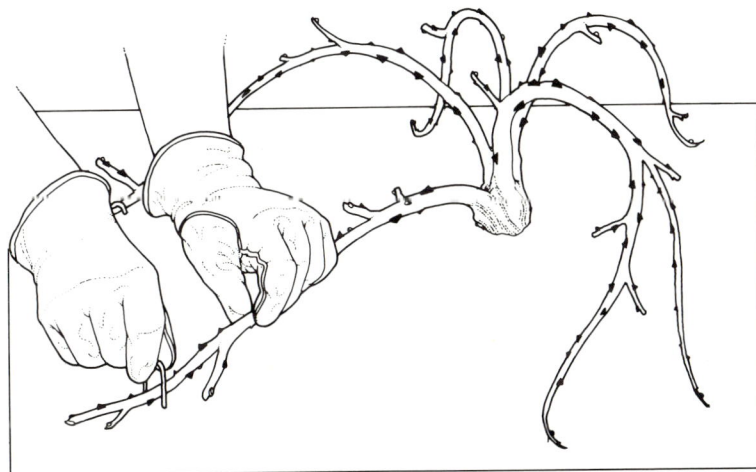

If you want to use a rose for ground cover, this is the way you spread out the branches and pin them down.

GROUND COVER FOR ROSES

We must now consider the vexed question of whether we may have ground cover amongst our roses, that is to say, whether it is permissible to plant amongst the bedded out Hybrid Tea and Floribunda roses?

Shrub and old-fashioned roses

I think it is wholly permissible to have ground cover amongst the shrub and old-fashioned roses. One does not often see them in separate beds anyway, but here and there amongst the other shrubs.

Of course not all combinations work: a clump of yellow heathers amongst the Centifolias or the Damask moss roses, for instance, would not feel at all right to me—but you will obviously choose carefully the places in the border for your old roses. For ground cover around them use the hardy geranium, especially as it will add a blue note. Some of the darker creeping conifers would help to clothe the ground around them in the winter, and why not have lilies-of-the-valley running through? *Alchemilla mollis* has a nice old-fashioned look, and with greenish yellow flowers goes happily with any colour. Campanulas and Nepeta are blue again, while the silver of Santolina and *Stachys lanata* makes a wonderful foil for the pinks of the old roses. And what about the bronze-purple of Ajuga—a great contrast to pink—and those tiny pansies (*Viola cornuta*) which will climb in and out of so many things in the summer.

Edging in the rose garden

Now let us look at the rose garden 'proper'. One thing we can do without annoying anyone is to edge it—and the edging can be permanent and perennial. Here I am only going to make suggestions, because just as the roses in the beds will be individual choices, so no doubt will the edging. In any case I am in favour of a neutral-coloured edging, but if the beds contain some of the new very bright orange or vermilion-red roses ('Duke of Windsor', for instance), then a quiet-coloured edge is essential.

If it is to be a shrubby edging dwarf lavender, Cotton lavender cotton (Santolina) and box are the sort of plants to use; trim them as a miniature hedge. If perennial plants are decided upon, pinks (Dianthus) are good because, though the flowering season is short, the grey leaves are formal if kept very tidily. Thrift is good for the same reason. *Cineraria maritima*, in some of its named varieties, will be perennial in some milder areas and needs to be kept neatly uniform. *Anaphalis triplinervis*—the shorter kind—is good. So is Erigeron, but get a blue one and not a pink. *Aster* × *frikartii* will flower for a long period and bring blue to your bed. Dwarf sedums are splendid even when not in flower. Many of the lower-growing herbs would also be suitable, the various thymes and sages, for example—try the purple-leaved sage with red and orange roses. Chives look similar to thrift when in flower and are good for keeping greenfly away. Pansies are excellent; again they bring blue to the bed and will flower the whole season if you dead-head them and trim them. *Asperula odorata*, Sweet woodruff, has white flowers and fresh green tufts of foliage. London pride (*Saxifraga umbrosa*) is also a good edger.

Under-planting your rose beds

So much for edging—only suggestions of course. The rose beds need certain attentions during the year, and that is why some purists demand that you should not plant ground cover under them. In a small garden this is an awful waste of space and in a large garden it is a waste of labour. Please be careful with any under-planting and respect where the rose roots are—nothing too deep or disturbing.

If you do your pruning in late March one could have a display of the small dwarf species tulips first. *Tulipa turkestanica* might be the earliest and has several heads to each bulb. *T. kaufmanniana* and *T. greigii*, which has mottled and striped leaves, will follow. Forget-me-nots will make a mist of blue amongst the new red foliage of the roses. All this you can clear away for the annual feeding, and then plant out later in the season with large drifts of petunias.

All plants are happier close together and in company, and this is another reason why I advocate under-planting a rose bed. You might just as well have it full of colourful plants as full of weeds which you have to keep culling. Also—and this gladdens my heart—if you under-plant you will not be able to use weed-killers.

For the last five years, for the gardens I have designed for London's Capital Radio for the Chelsea Flower Show, Messrs Suttons of Torquay have supplied me with mostly annual flowers, and most greatly admired have been their pansies—named varieties of different colours, ranging from white through yellow and apricot (this is a really fabulous colour) to rust colour and dark, velvety pansy red-maroon, from light blue to dark blue and almost navy blue—and, of course, blue is the one colour to aim at with roses. So, shall we say you have a dozen beds with a dozen roses in each, each bed containing the same rose, you could choose your colour to suit your roses and have pansies in each bed. There is a particular dwarf nasturtium that they do with dark foliage and crimson flowers called 'Red Roulette', which makes a memorable ground cover for very bright roses like 'Duke of Windsor'.

Under white roses like 'Iceberg' or 'Pascali' the variegated hostas are very effective. (It is perhaps better not to let them flower.) One of their advantages is that they disappear in autumn, allowing you to prune and fertilize in the spring—but be careful then for the new shoots are fleshy and tender. *Hosta fortunei picta*, *H. crispula* and *H.* 'Thomas Hogg' are the best variegated ones. The 'Papa Meilland' rose is the darkest of reds and the bush is naturally tallish and upright; amongst a group of these roses you could grow that most sumptuous of hostas (with its ribbed leaves explaining its other name of Plantain lily), *H. sieboldiana elegans*, with almost blue leaves and the palest violet flowers fading to white. Yellow or pale orange roses would be enhanced by the yellowish green leaves of *H. fortunei aurea*. With a bed of roses like 'Mountbatten' (a strong yellow), 'Can-Can' (strong vermilion with dark purple foliage), 'Vital Spark' (orangy-yellow double Floribunda), 'Super Star' (light vermilion) or 'Fragrant Cloud' (coral-red), Ajuga—the Bugle, which creeps and covers everywhere with its shiny coppery-purple leaves— makes a very effective colour contrast.

Another annual with similar colouring, with bronzy purple serrated leaves, is *Perilla* 'Atropurpurea Laciniata', offered by Bees and Suttons. This is a half-hardy annual, a bedding plant pure and simple, and as it is 2 feet (60cm) high it needs to be planted under tallish roses. Use it under a bed of pink roses like 'Prima Ballerina'— which to my mind is one of the most hardy, showy, beautifully perfumed roses, and it will flower generously for the whole season. *Salvia horminum* (Clary) 'Bluebeard' has strongly coloured floral leaves or bracts and will flower from July onwards. It is 18 inches (45cm) high and makes a glorious foil to pink roses. This is a hardy annual; grown in peat pots in a frame, it need not be planted out until all pruning and fertilizing is over.

The grey leaves of *Hebe pinguifolia pagei* form a dense, low mat;

'Mountbatten' is a new, tall floribunda that was used in the Princess of Wales' wedding bouquet.

the white flowers are earlier than the roses, and as this is an evergreen shrub it is a permanent planting. Being grey it will go well with any colour rose, and being so near the ground even low-spreading bushes like 'Josephine Bruce' (a deep dark crimson which would go very well with the grey) will not be overwhelmed.

Rock roses have shrubby foliage and need to be 'gone over' with the shears after flowering, but they are evergreen and, so long as you choose the right colours, will make a very useful ground cover for rose beds. They prefer full sun and a not too heavy soil. Possibly the most vigorous kind is *Helianthemum appeninum roseum*, which has pink double flowers. 'Wisley Primrose' and 'Wisley Pink' both have grey foliage.

Acaena 'Blue Haze' is low-growing with fern-like foliage; this is excellent for low-growing roses like 'Typhoon', and it is the right colour, too. Another silver sub-shrub which needs a kindly climate and a well-drained bed is the *Convolvulus Cneorum*—which Hugh Johnson says is as lovely as a bride. It certainly is, and as innocent-looking. Each plant (put them fairly close together) forms an evergreen hummock of silver silky leaves, and it blooms all summer through, with the palest of silver-pink flowers. There is none of the trailing one would expect from a bindweed, but it needs a lot of sun and in a harsher climate it will need the protection of a cold frame in the winter. *Stachys lanata* (Lamb's-lugs) will also enhance pink roses with a carpet of silver leaves.

For carpeting beneath pale pink or white roses why not try the variegated strawberry, with its half cream and half green leaves?

Rosa 'Handel' with *Stachys lanata*. **The neutral greys and silvers enhance the colour of the roses.**

There are also several herbs which can be used as ground cover—
I have already mentioned some for edging. There are four sages:
Salvia officinalis, the ordinary grey sage from the kitchen garden, *S.
o. purpurascens*, the purple-leaved one; *S. o. icterina*, a yellow
variegated form; and *S. o. tricolor*, which is white and pink and
greenish grey. Why not form beds of equal size, each carpeted with a
different sage and each containing a different kind of Hybrid Tea
rose of similar height. And all edged with, shall we say, Santolina—
the idea of the common edging being to give a completeness to the
whole. (By the way, do not try to grow rue near the sage or the sage
will wither—they do not make happy neighbours.) Rue would make
excellent ground cover on its own away from sage, and would I think
be very effective indeed with yellow roses like 'Midas', 'Grandpa
Dickson' or 'Princess Michael of Kent'. Variegated pineapple mint
is the only mint I would use—how good this would look with a
bluish rose like 'Blue Moon' or 'Godfrey Winn'. The other mints are
too vigorous and intrusive. The golden marjoram, *Origanum
vulgare aureum*, spreads vigorously and is excellent for our purpose.

Thyme came first to England in Elizabethan times, so it will
certainly look well with any of the old shrub roses. There is the
lemon-scented thyme, with its silvery leaves, and the gilded thyme
Thymus × citriodorus aureus, with a scent of balm and golden leaf
markings. *Thymus fragrantissima* has a fragrance of oranges. Bees
delight in the flowers of thyme, most of which are purple, pinky or
mauve, borne in conical clusters from June until September. Being a
Mediterranean sub-shrub it does like to be in well drained soil and in
the sun. Plant it closely in the rose bed and you will have a complete
carpet—good with dark red or yellow roses but not with pink or
orange ones. If you do not want to carpet a bed with thyme, put them
in the crevices of the flagstones round the rose beds: step on them
and enhance the perfume of the whole garden.

Under pink or white roses another lovely herb to use is basil—the
dark opal variety (*Ocimum basilicum*). It has very dark bronze,
almost black leaves with a very dark pink-cum-mauve flower. It is
nicely bushy and an easily grown half-hardy annual. It grows 16
inches (40cm) tall so can only be used with tall roses, but there is a
dwarf variety that was used by the Elizabethans as an edging plant.

*   *   *

I know this has nothing to do with roses and ground cover but it has
to do with the juxtapositioning of roses and complementary plants.
Edward Hyams, a great gardener and garden writer, alas now dead,
had in his Devonshire gardens *Buddleia* 'Lochinch'—a summer-
flowering shrub with richly fragrant, almost true blue flowers with
an orange eye, felted white shoots and young leaves of silver—next
to a *Rosa soulieana* which has fine grey-green leaves and multitudes
of single white flowers with yellow stamens which completely
smother the leaves when it is flowering, grows to 10 feet (3m) high,
and again is highly fragrant. Mr Hyams no doubt did not suffer from
hay-fever—but it is this enormous concentration of scent which I
find overwhelmingly lovely in a garden.

5

Hybrid Teas, Floribundas and Miniature Roses

The Hybrid Tea is far and away the most popular rose today. It is perfect casting (as we would say in the theatre) for the modern small garden, especially for bedding out.

HYBRID TEAS

I think if you said 'Rose?' to ninety-nine people in the street, in their mind's eye they would see a Hybrid Tea-shaped bloom, with its big, conical, shapely flowers enhanced by its outside 'peeling' back reflex petals. Jack Harkness calls it the 'present climax of thousands of years of loving and growing roses'.

One can think back many years. In the same way that some people will lie back in front of the logs of a slow-burning apple wood fire and savour a majestic claret drunk many years ago on their palate's memory, so one can think back on some glorious roses, hardly grown in today's gardens. I can remember Christopher Stone, not only for his mellow voice and civilized humour as the first ever disc jockey, but I can remember the rose named after him, introduced in 1935, scarlet over-laid crimson in colour, with a bloom of rich damasky fragrance and velvet texture. But, unlike the claret which has gone for ever, one can come across in some neglected gardens, or in the corner of some rosarian connoisseur's far plot, a sudden forgotten bush filling the air generously with its scent and sunning itself serenely for my *present* pleasure. I can also remember my grandfather in his tiny back garden in Watford, growing one of the first apricot-cum-orange roses, 'Daily Mail'. This won a competition in the 1920s, and he felt a very up-to-date gardener because he had one. There is a brand new Hybrid Tea today, 'Camphill Glory', which is a similar shade, perhaps paler, if I can rely upon the memory of a

Right: 'Silver Jubilee' is an excellent example of a modern Hybrid Tea. Its shape and colour are good, and it is fairly fragrant.

48

small boy of seven or eight. The name of this rose commemorates the work of the Camphill Village Trust; the Trust receives a donation for each rose sold by Harkness, who introduced it.

Another rose that has a strong hold on my affections—I have already mentioned it I'm sure several times— is 'Papa Meilland'. It was introduced by A. Meilland of France in 1963, and is sadly prone to mildew. It is a large, full rose of dark velvety crimson, rich with fragrance. Its petals, though so dark in colour, are shaded—or the sun upon them makes them look as if each petal is of a different darkness. I brought one into the house to please my father when he was very ill, and I believe it was the last piece of this world's beauty that he enjoyed.

'Prima Ballerina' I have also mentioned in other chapters. To my mind this is the perfect Hybrid Tea pink rose—yet it was introduced as long ago as 1958 by Tantau. It is shapely, its fragrance is outstanding, and it is very strong in the stem. I had a couple of dozen of them in a sentinel row on my terrace in Sussex; it acted as a sort of hedge to soften the outlines of a balustrade, and as the balustrade edged the terrace which exploited the view—12 miles (19km) south to the sea, and 30 or 40 miles (48–64km) to the west, whence came the prevailing winds, sometimes of gale force—you will see what an accommodating ballet dancer she is, and aptly named for this reason. Sometimes in my pantomimes, where we employed dancers straight from the Royal Ballet School, those strong little ladies would be playing two performances daily—which means six hours in front of the public—and they would still come to practise and limber up at ballet classes in the mornings! I shall expect a new introduction in 1982–3 from Peter Beales to be of similar constitution: 'Anna Pavlova', named after the famous prima ballerina. Here is the description from the catalogue by Keith Money, who has written a biography of the great lady: 'There is a real period charm about the full, slightly frilled petals with their shades of face-powder pink, all set off with the darkest possible leaves, strangely circular. The scent of this rose sets it apart—I cannot think of another rose like it. It is quite haunting; the nearest I can get to describing it would be to imagine a picnic of fresh fruit salad, topped with Turkish Delight and served under a flowering May tree!'

Let us consider the vermilion-reds and oranges and deep yellows in the Hybrid Teas. I have already explained how the first yellow Hybrid Tea, 'Soleil d'Or', was discovered by M. Pernet-Ducher, the French nurseryman (see p. 19). He then crossed this back to the Austrian Copper rose, *R. foetida bicolor*, and the seedlings from this were a very strong orange and a deep yellow. The Austrian Copper, says Mr Humphrey Brooke (and many other authorities), is the reason for the spread of blackspot amongst modern roses. He says that at Sangerhausen, the rose garden in East Germany, it has been possible to eliminate all spraying against blackspot in the 25 acres (10 hectares) of their rosarium since hybrids of Austrian Copper parentage were sent into remote exile.

A. Sigston Thompson, former Honorary Director of Gardens, Harlow Car Gardens, Harrogate, wrote in the *Rose Annual* of 1977:

A selection of Hybrid Teas:
Top left: 'Wendy Cussons'.
Left: 'Papa Meilland'.
Bottom left: 'Double Delight'
Top right: 'Troika'.
Above right: 'Dutch Gold'.

'And our Hybrid Teas consist of 2 rows growing in what I consider to be the only proper place for Hybrid Teas, in the Kitchen Garden, so that my wife can have a few to cut for the house.' Now I really must find a worthy authority to contradict that. Hugh Johnson, in one of the best all-round gardening books I know and certainly one of the most beautiful, *The Principles of Gardening* (Mitchell Beazley, 1979), says: 'And certainly among man-made flowers, there is nothing more sensuous than a modern rose bud . . . they are supremely graceful and may never be surpassed.'

So much for each classically shaped rose. Now how do we use them in the garden? We have agreed, I think, that the Hybrid Tea is usually a rather stiff, formal plant. It has to be to present its classic shapes and colours with sufficient panache. We know, too, that each bush grows to a formalized height and shape; not like the shrub roses which are rampant, haphazard growers, in one garden a giant, in another reasonably sized. Each year we prune the Hybrid Tea to the shape and size we require. In short, it is the ideal plant for what the Victorians called 'bedding-out', to use at regular intervals in regularly shaped beds. There is no other shrub or plant which has such remarkable permanency in the garden, which has such an extraordinarily long flowering season, which does not need staking; but which does need pruning, spraying, dead-heading and fertilizing. When, however, you see its unparalleled return, it is surely worth these ministrations.

The bed of 'Silver Jubilee' shown on p. 49 proves my point most eloquently. As we all know, the rose was bred by Cockers to celebrate the Queen's Silver Jubilee. The shapely blooms are of pink, peach and cream, and most subtly blended. It could be described as silver and apricot. The foliage is glossy and disease-resistant, and how uniformly it stands.

Choice is always very personal with flowers, and indeed most works of art. I have chosen a dozen Hybrid Teas: all of them please me; some have been on the market for some time and some are new. We have already made a start with my two favourites, 'Papa Meilland' and 'Prima Ballerina'.

'**Duke of Windsor**' is a startling vermilion-red. Some might call it a dark orange. It is of medium height, prolific of bloom, fragrant and healthy. It carries an armoury of big thorns.

'**Peace**' is the rose everyone knows. It is a very vigorous bush; everything about it is large. It has full-petalled blooms of yellow with a reddish flush, strong, branching growth, and leathery dark green foliage. Not strongly fragrant, but enough to be included by me.

'**King's Ransom**' Rich yellow, fragrant blooms; upright growth to about 2 feet 6 inches (75cm) high.

'**Ernest H. Morse**' Turkey-red blooms, very fragrant and free-flowering; about 4 feet (1.2m).

'**Pristine**' White and scented. Long pointed buds open to a large bloom of white shaded light pink with good weather resistance. Very free-flowering, with upright growth to 3 feet (90cm) or so. Large dark green leaves.

'**Piccadilly**' Brilliant scarlet blooms with yellow blush. This is an early flowerer and repeats quickly. Upright in growth, the same size roughly as the last two roses. Regrettably it has very little scent, but a bi-colour as outstanding as this really must be grown.

'**Double Delight**' This is also a bi-colour, but this one is fragrant. It has many-petalled flowers that are a blend of ivory and cherry-red, upright growth, and mid-green foliage; it is taller than the last few. For goodness sake do not plant it near to 'Piccadilly'. The colour clash would send you screaming from the garden.

'**Fragrant Cloud**' Reckoned to be very fragrant, this has large well-formed flowers of deep coral-red. Very free-flowering with abundant dark green foliage. A bit susceptible to blackspot with me.

'**Wendy Cussons**' Very fragrant, cerise blooms, perfectly formed, and a branching habit. See the fabulous picture of the bed of bushes and standards in Regents Park on page 96. Medium height.

'**Just Joey**' Large, fragrant blooms of deep copper, very attractive when fully open. It is free-flowering, with semi-branching habit and deep green foliage. Medium height.

*   *   *

What a uniform splash of colour a bed of Hybrid Teas makes in the garden. A positive treasure trove of non-fading roses. We now have this picture, a pageant of flaming roses mingling their perfumes on a summer evening—especially the late summer's extravagant flush, which is usually of a deeper colour than the midsummer one because the jealous sun has not claimed the colour from its rival quite so demandingly.

Every garden must have a climax, usually emphasized by intensity of light or depth of shadow, and most readily achieved by an emphasis on strong colour and scent. The Hybrid Tea rose is the best way to do this—certainly for the length of time it can be held, for in a garden all is change.

FLORIBUNDA ROSES

It is old-fashioned of me to talk about Hybrid Tea roses and Floribunda roses today. I have done so to avoid confusion, because so many catalogues, and so many garden centres and professional gardeners and television pundits, still use this nomenclature.

The roses previously known as Hybrid Teas should now be called Large Flowered Roses, while those roses known as Floribundas should now be called Cluster Roses. Both lots together are called Modern Roses, to distinguish them from the old shrub roses, which are now best described as Old Garden Roses, Modern Shrubs and Species Roses. You may think it a little quaint of me to mention these important facts so late on in this book, but I do so now as we have become better acquainted, and in a leisurely, meandering book of this kind I do not want to surprise you or to confuse.

I have already told you how these Cluster-cum-Floribunda roses came about (see chapter 1). Although the modern tendency is to make them look more and more like Hybrid Teas (some roses are left in a limbo of indecision and no one really knows which group to place them in), the Floribunda may be single, semi-double, double, shaped like a rosette ('Iceberg') or like a Hybrid Tea.

Because the Floribunda has more heads at the end of one stem than a Hybrid Tea, it has a longer period in bloom (the centre bud usually opens first and is followed by the smaller buds clustering around it). For this reason, and because usually it has a smaller number of petals, the Floribunda does better in a wet period: there are more buds to follow on, and the petals being formed do not 'ball-up' as a Hybrid Tea of many, many petals like 'Blue Moon' will do.

The one Floribunda I could not do without is '**Iceberg**'. It flowers the summer through, and it will either sit daintily in a mixed shrub border or make a magnificent bed of its own. The weather hardly affects it at all, and if you need a white, constantly flowering rose to help out a border of old shrub roses then 'Iceberg' will not look out of place. It also makes an excellent hedge. Many of the Floribundas do. It grows to 4 feet (1.2m) tall, and is good for cutting.

'**Rob Roy**' is a very good Hybrid Tea-type Floribunda of rich crimson. Slightly fragrant.

'**Korresia**' Bright yellow, a good unfading colour for bedding. It has given an outstanding show wherever I have seen it this summer. It is medium height, and fairly fragrant.

'**Harry Edland**' A very fragrant lilac rose. 3 feet (90cm).

'**City of Leeds**' Healthy semi-double salmon pink. This gave me great pleasure when I saw it in the garden at Bone Hill. To my mind this is almost fragrant! The effectiveness of this rose comes from the shapely salmon blooms against the dark bronzy green foliage.

'**Iced Ginger**' The colour is a blend of buff, copper, yellow and ivory, or cream shaded gingery pink! A bi-colour with a fair fragrance.

'**Greensleeves**' Clear Chartreuse-green flowers open out from pink-tinged buds. Not very fragrant I'm afraid, but it's a very pleasant and unusual novelty.

'**Margaret Merril**' Whenever I have seen this—at Chelsea, at the RNRS grounds at Bone Hill, at Bees Nursery at Chester or in Regents Park—I have been much attracted to what at first you think is a pure white Hybrid Tea-type rose. You then realize there is a faint, faint, shell-pink tinge to the interior of the full, very fragrant bloom. Harkness, the breeder, says: 'It creates a sensation of sweetness and contentment whenever the innocent pearly blush petals unfold.' Do you know, I believe it does!

'**News**' I make much of this rose, which I saw on my visit to Bone Hill, in a later chapter (see p. 85). It is an unusual colour, difficult for the printed page to portray. It is purple; it is beetroot-red in its bud stage. When you know its parentage (which is unusual enough— 'Lilac Charm' × 'Tuscany Superb'), then you can begin to imagine the colour is a mixture of the two. It is a vigorous rose over a long period, and fragrant.

Some Floribunda roses.
Left: A bed of 'News' at Bone
Hill—a glorious misty purple.
Top: 'Margaret Merril', which
according to Jack Harkness
'creates a sensation of
sweetness and contentment'.
Above: 'Korresia',
a bright unfading yellow.

Three miniature roses from the RNRS garden at Bone Hill.
Top Left: 'Little Flirt'. Above: 'Gold Coin'. Left: 'Scarlet Gem'.

'**Pink Parfait**' is a lovely rose, fragrant, shapely and healthy. It is a medium pink with a yellow base to the petals (a little like 'Peace' might be described, the other way round!). It is prolific in flower right through the season, and very weather-resistant. Medium height, with semi-glossy foliage.

'**Court Jester**' In colour it would roughly take the place of the 'Duke of Windsor' in a Hybrid Tea collection. It is very tall, and the blooms are of a bright golden orange with a yellow reverse. A bi-colour with dark green foliage.

'**English Miss**' is very fragrant, with light pink blooms that are especially effective in contrast to the purplish, dark green foliage. The pink is very pale, a salmony shell colour in its interior shadows. Medium height.

* * *

So there are twelve Floribundas. As you will see, they all flower over a very long period, with a great number of flowers. They are all pretty healthy, but if they lack anything they lack fragrance—and to me this is one of the essences of a rose. It is quite obvious that the Large Flowered Roses and the Cluster Roses will produce amongst each other better roses that are healthier, more floriferous, and in more unusual colours—and let's have more scent. No other shrub has so many people so busily refining it as the rose has. All for yours and my delight.

MINIATURE ROSES

Miniature roses are becoming increasingly popular for several reasons. Gardens are getting smaller all the time, and through the media knowledge of miniature roses is growing. With the cult of the window box for flats, the suitability of the miniature rose for growing in window boxes has increased the demand for them. House plants are also becoming more and more popular, and—quite wrongly—people think that a miniature rose in a pot is a splendid addition to their collection. Sadly the miniature rose will only be happy indoors for a very short time, and could not live there permanently. Another reason for their popularity is possibly that one can easily propagate them from cuttings, and amateur growers love this, not only to increase their own stock but also to give away as a most pleasant present for friends.

How did they begin? The first account, possibly apocryphal, is that a tiny rose imported from China (*R. chinensis minima*) to the island of Mauritius, circa 1810, later came to England. This got lost or forgotten, however, and there is virtually no known rose today which bears the name *R. chinensis minima*. Then one day—quite by chance apparently—in 1917 in Switzerland a Colonel Roulet, officer in the Swiss Army, told his friend Henry Correvon, a rose grower of Geneva, of a miniature rose growing in pots on a windowsill in a Swiss village. In 1922 Correvon introduced *R. rouletii*—a miniature rose with pink double flowers; he thought of calling it 'Pompon de Paris', but decided to name it after the Colonel.

We now move to Holland—to Boskoop where John de Vink had a nursery. In 1935 he raised a seedling which he named 'Peon', with deep crimson flowers with a white eye. Others followed: 'Pixie' (pink), 'Cinderella' (white), 'Oakington Ruby', etc. 'Peon' was bred from *R. rouletii* and 'Gloria Mundi'. And in Spain, in 1940, Pedro Dot, a world-famous rose breeder whose speciality was brilliantly coloured Hybrid Teas, bred the first miniature yellow rose by crossing *R. rouletii* with a Hybrid Tea. It was called 'Baby Gold Star', followed by 'Rosina', also a brilliant yellow.

The most prominent breeder of miniatures in the world today is an American, Ralph Moore of California (represented in this country by Gregory's of Nottingham). McGredy (Ireland), Meilland (France) and Kordes (Germany) are also now working on miniatures. 'Starina' (1965) and 'Darling Flame' (1971) have both come from Meilland.

Miniature roses range in height from 6 to 18 inches (15–45cm), with blooms $\frac{1}{2}$–$1\frac{1}{2}$ inches ($1\frac{1}{2}$–4cm) in diameter. Anyone can grow them. They are perfectly hardy out of doors—though a severe frost will force the roots upwards from the ground, and they must be firmed in again. I remember last autumn, quite late in the season, Tony Gregory brought a whole lot of miniatures—at least a couple of dozen different varieties—to show on our TV programme for CCT in Birmingham. He said he had brought them from the field that morning, where they had been sparkling with frost in the early morning sun. They were wonderfully healthy and made a magical item for the programme. The miniatures are susceptible to the usual rose pests, as I found in my Sussex garden, particularly to blackspot—but there again these were yellow blooms.

Miniatures can be grown as a border to larger roses, or in rockeries—especially some of the new trailing and climbing varieties—stone troughs, pots, etc. Window boxes planted with these dainty roses will flower most of the summer—keep dead-heading them, of course. Or you can make a feature of them in strawberry pots. Use a good rich loam, with added rotted farmyard manure and fish meal. Most varieties root from cuttings in a mist propagator, greenhouse or frame, or hardwood cuttings can be taken in the late summer. Put them in a sandy trench, as with other hardwood cuttings, over-winter in a frame, plant out in the spring, and they will bloom that summer. A slip with a heel is good, but the best way is from a straight cutting with a split stem dipped in a hormone rooting powder.

Miniature roses come as bushes, standards and climbers (a good climber is the pale pearl-pink, almost white, 'Nozomi'). There are now miniature Moss roses as well. 'Fairy Moss' was introduced by Ralph Moore in 1969 (one of its ancestors was 'William Lobb'); it is rose-red, while 'Dresden Doll', also introduced by Ralph Moore, is a double pink. I find these tiny dolls' house Moss roses absolutely enchanting, and though they are often victims of blackspot it is worth spending any amount of time spraying them.

A good place for the climbers is at the base of a low drystone wall, or at the top of a drystone retaining wall to drift down over the edge. Or why not use a climbing miniature rose like 'Red Cascade' in a hanging basket? Or plant up a window box with a good lavender one like 'Lavender Lace', together with 'Dresden Doll' and the new unusual green varieties 'Green Ice' and 'Green Diamond'. The green here is a soft colour, a real green sheen on a proper rose bloom—nothing like the old *R. chinensis* 'Viridiflora'.

I also have an idea—and someone must try this—of using miniature roses (particularly the denser-growing ones that are only 8–10 inches (20–25cm) high) as the main ingredient of a parterre bed. The tiny contents of the bed demand that it should be small, shall we say 3 feet wide by 9 feet long (90cm × 2.7m). Copy a scroll design from one of the great gardens—why not Versailles or Hampton Court? You could get the design, perhaps an original Le Notre, for the cost of a postcard!

*   *   *

A couple of Chelsea Flower Shows ago it was brought to my notice that there was a rose named after Anna Ford and another after Angela Rippon; the team spirit engendered by *That's Life* made me think that there should be one named after Esther Rantzen. I had a word with Jack Harkness. 'Of course', he said, 'Get Esther to come along and choose one of our new seedlings.' When she came back she said, 'It's gorgeous. It's a miniature with a rose-red flower. Quite beautiful!' 'So we now have an Esther Rantzen rose,' I said. 'No,' she said, 'I've called it Esther's Baby!' It has bright rose-red flowers, with two rows of petals—the inner one offset against the outer to charming effect. It is a leafy, spreading plant and in my Sussex garden it flowered all summer long, and right into the autumn. The Harkness catalogues put it amongst the cluster-flowered Floribunda bush roses, and say it's 18 inches (45cm) high. It was not as high as this with me, and the size of its flowers still makes me think of it as a miniature. I've a new miniature then! So has Esther, only hers is called Emily Alice.

'Esther's Baby', the 18-inch (45cm) high rose named after Esther Rantzen's baby, Emily Alice.

6

Old Shrub Roses

Are you a romantic? Do you like to take yourself back in time and fantasize? Would this be growing here? And how would an old knot garden look? Are ancient Dutchmen looking at me over this bed of modern tulips that are nearly black? Is this perhaps the fascination of the stately home? In our minds we banish the crowds, the emptying coachload of people, the child which is wiping its ice-cream down our trousers, and in our imagination we go back and exist for moments of joy in another dimension. Apart from their own particular beauty and their wonderful scent, this is the allure of the old shrub roses. I am quite sure this is what Vita Sackville-West was playing at when she, of ancient aristocratic lineage, created her garden of enchantment round the ruined castle tower at Sissinghurst. Not for her the garishly modern rhododendron, the flashy Floribunda or the Hybrid Tea. For her there were back-drops of yew hedges, and beds neatly carved into almost parterre shapes with little hedges of box—and the greatest feature of all in her garden? The old roses. Glorious old climbers nodding their hot summer days against a sun-baked wall of old bricks. The muted colours are burgundy-purple, shell-pink, smoky lavender, pale lilac, and pink with a silver satin sheen. The shapes are gloriously relaxed; they are rounded, flat, cupped, bell-like. They do not poke their conical perfect-shaped noses at you like the Hybrid Teas do; they loll; their stems are soft and hardly able to bear the weight of all this beauty, so that the heads fall shyly before you. And all the time they are so generous with their scent that the summer's afternoon is heavy with it, and the bees, intoxicated with it, mingle their contented buzzing, so that scent and sound are almost one. If we look at a picture we are looking into a romantic world of make-believe; even if the picture is of some well-known scene it is a moment caught in time. This is the way to look at a garden, and this is why the old shrub roses are so

Right: Typical of the old shrub roses is 'President de Sèze', a Gallica introduced in 1836, with heavily scented 4-inch (10cm) blooms.

valuable to you, the gardener.

I think the best way to use these roses is in the shrub border, and in special positions in the garden, sometimes as a focal point. The climbers are very welcome on the house, or on a garden wall. If you have a retaining wall perhaps 3 feet (90cm) or so high, here is an excellent place for a shrub rose. It will have the shelter of the wall, and if it is a straggling, floppy type of shrub the wall will give it excellent natural support when it is tied in to it. A white shrub rose is an excellent way to keep clashing colours apart in the shrub border. A shrub rose is also effective against a pillar. I had a 'Maigold' rose against a pillar which was exactly right in shape and form. It was fragrant and it flowered twice a summer.

The 1980 edition of the *Rose Annual* reported on a symposium where a distinguished panel voted on the twelve best Bourbon and Hybrid Perpetual roses. Typically these are 5–6 feet (1.5–1.8m) tall and a good 3 feet (90cm) across, well branched but generally upright, flowering twice a year, in June/July and again in September. In all the members of the panel chose forty-three varieties.

Position	Variety	Points
1	Mme Isaac Pereire (B)	16
2	Reine des Violettes (HP)	14
	Zéphirine Drouhin (B)	14
4	Mme Pierre Oger (B)	13
	Mrs John Laing (HP)	13
6	Ferdinand Pichard (HP)	11
7	Boule de Neige (B)	10
	La Reine Victoria (B)	10
9	Kathleen Harrop (B)	9
10	Baron Girod de l'Ain (HP)	8
	Louise Odier (B)	8
	Souvenir de la Malmaison (B)	8

'Zéphirine Drouhin' I know well as it has graced two of my dark grey stone walls in Sussex for several years. No rose was more vigorous, it was frequently early, I never sprayed it in a viciously blackspot area, and it seemed always to have some flowers in between its two very fine flowering periods of June and September. Next to it was a *Ceanothus* 'Gloire de Versailles', and in front was one of those mop-headed hydrangeas that never knew if its flowers were pink or blue or a marvellous grey-green—there would be some florets containing all colours, and it hid the sometimes bare base of the rose. To the left was the largest and tallest of the Anaphalis (*A. yedoensis*), and a large clump of tall Michaelmas daisies—*Aster novae-belgii*—the darkest navy blue, and I'm afraid I do not know his name; Admiral somebody I'd think! It was a lovely corner with its strong pink rose and the grey of the stone and the different blues—by the time the silver of the Anaphalis was dominant the

Opposite: 'Zéphirine Drouhin', a Bourbon, famous, fragrant and fabulous. A climber, and the experts' second choice.

ceanothus was on its autumnal stint of flowering, which used to carry on well into November. This rose was introduced in 1868, and for it to take second place in this list after all these years was a great credit to it. It is often called thornless: mine wasn't, but it had a strong, refreshing fragrance.

The first rose to flower with me is *R. primula*—I have it against a grey stone wall. It is never taller than me and it has scented fern-like foliage on red stems; the flowers are primrose in shape and colour. As I turn the corner in spring I always smile, it is impossible to see this rose without doing so—and, of course, it smiles back. I first planted it at the foot of a pergola pillar (which was stupid anyway as I thought then it would grow higher). This pillar was at the edge of my dog run and my English setter used to browse on it; she never allowed it to grow to more than a foot (30cm) high, and I had to wait until the autumn to move it. Was it the scented foliage she liked the taste of? Other than the odd blade of grass for medicinal purposes I have never known her eat any other plant in the garden.

A Hybrid Musk rose which has given me a lot of pleasure is 'Pink Prosperity'. The bush is 5 feet (1.5m) high and 4 feet (1.2m) wide. The stems are dark red and slightly mossy, mostly near the flower. It has large trusses of scented, cup-like, double flowers of clear bright pink, fading to a pastel shade of pink, almost white; when half open they appear like many miniature roses in a bunch. It flowers strongly again in the autumn. I planted mine against a low wall, over which fell in great profusion the ferny leaves and white daisy flowers of *Anthemis cupaniana*, a huge hummock of it. The flowers were over and neatly trimmed off (they really smell quite horribly if allowed to die and disintegrate!) by the time the pink of the roses was seen against it—one plant enhancing another as one tries so hard to do in the garden. For a lot of people *A. cupaniana* is too vigorous and intrusive, but if you are firm with it, its grey ferny leaves are indispensable.

'Reine des Violettes' is a Hybrid Perpetual and was equal second with 'Zéphirine Drouhin' on the experts' list. It is a rich purple, double, quartered, flat, open rose, which fades to a lilac-mauve when fully open. It has also been described as being of a soft grape purple. This is considered the bluest rose ever raised, but it is too mauve, too lilac, too violet, ever to give me a hint of blue. There is obviously blue pigment there, but it does not in any way look an 'un-roselike' colour as 'Godfrey Winn' or 'Blue Moon' do. (Incidentally 'Blue Moon' is a fabulous rose for its perfume alone— I wish its stems were not so feeble!) The greyish green leaves form a perfect foil for the flowers. It also has a fantastic fragrance. It needs hard pruning in February to ensure its continuous flowering, and plenty of food with that in mind as well. It can be used as a climber, and this helps to expose the flowers, which have a tendency to 'hide' amongst the foliage.

Until I owned it, I was inclined to confuse 'Reine des Violettes' in books and chat with 'Violette', a rose introduced in 1921 which flowers early in the rambler season. It is misnamed in that its flowers are a crimson-purple, but they do fade to maroon-purple and they were certainly this colour when I met it at Hidcote—doubly beautiful as it tumbled over the honey-coloured Cotswold stone wall of the forecourt. It smells of apples and is quite enchanting. It is at Nymans, Sussex, too.

A digression on shrubs

I am going to digress here and think of as many shrubs as possible which complement the shrub roses, ramblers and climbers. Rosemary and lavender immediately come to mind, both with greyish foliage and blue flowers. Clematis we have talked of as helping to extend the season and add blue to the climbers, ceanothus we have also mentioned. The blue lace-cap hydrangea is more delicately suitable than the mop-head, while a climbing hydrangea makes an excellent background for shrub roses. Yew could not be better, either in a solid dark hedge or as a topiary dome or suchlike. *Berberis × stenophylla* has flowered by the time the roses do and its dark spiny branches, falling gracefully forward, make it an excellent shrub to grow with roses. Lilac is always a problem in the garden; it is such a dark-foliaged lump once it has flowered. Have a semi-climbing shrub rose behind it and pull it over the lilac when it has finished flowering and before the rose does and you will have achieved as good a trick as Paul Daniel. Cotton lavender (*Santolina chamaecyparissus*) and the Curry plant (*Helichrysum italicum*) provide good greys to complement the pastel shades of the roses, as indeed does *Senecio laxifolius*. And what about a weeping Silver pear for a tall shrub rose to romp about and through? Some of the silver-leaved conifers also make excellent foils.

Copper-leaved shrubs and hedges give a depth of colour exactly

'William Lobb'—note the moss on the buds. I have to have this rose in every garden I make.

suited to make the delicacy of the shrub roses stand out. Many of the acers, both tree and shrub, could be considered. Imagine *Acer platanoides* 'Crimson King' with the deep violet-blue, double *Clematis* 'Vyvyan Pennell' climbing through it, together with the apricot-yellow cascade of a 'Climbing Lady Hillingdon'—which instead of being a lady of the manor with determinedly shod feet and an alpenstock is a lovely loosely double, gracious flower which Graham Stuart Thomas tells us has a 'delicious fragrance of a freshly opened packet of tea with a hint of apricots'. *Acer palmatum atropurpureum* is a graceful small shrub that will help a shrub rose rather than overwhelm it, while for a forward position, with the rose in the background, a mound of *A. palmatum dissectum atropurpureum* would make a pleasant picture. *Cotinus coggygria* 'Royal Purple' would make a nice contrast for a pink rose, while *Phormium tenax purpureum* might be effective as dramatic sentinels at the end of a border. To go with a climber on a wall—but be sure it does not overwhelm it—I suggest *Vitis vinifera purpurea*. A pink rose and this vine climbing through and hanging down from a *Pyrus salicifolia pendula* would make a group to remember. Plants are gregarious, and as well as looking spectacular together when rightly chosen they often flourish together better than when on their own. Another idea for a wall would be as early a pink climber as you can get ('May Queen'), together with *Wisteria sinensis* 'Black Dragon', which has double flowers of dark purple. Finally, *Rosa rubrifolia*, with its purple glaucous foliage, makes a good contrasting plant with other roses.

And now back to the roses

I love the dusky, hairy stems of a Moss rose (*R. centifolia muscosa*). Indeed I love the mysterious look of it altogether. The rose has a dense, moss-like, glandular-bristly covering on its stems, branches, petioles, flower-stalks and calyx tubes. This bristly covering is sticky to the touch, and when bruised gives off a resinous odour. The flowers are clear pink, globular and double, opening to a flat bloom which is richly scented like a vintage hock. There is a modern yellow called 'Golden Moss', but perhaps the most rewarding is 'Mousseline'. From June to October it bears large, cup-shaped, soft flesh-pink flowers, which are drenched with a sweet fragrance. I had one about 4 feet (1.2m) tall and 4 feet (1.2m) wide, growing on a stable wall near the entrance to the kitchen. All summer through 'Mousseline' flowered, and it seemed that towards the autumn the pink became a silver pink, especially in moonlight. Lobb is one of my favourite theatrical characters—in J. M. Barrie's *Dear Brutus* he is the mysterious genius in the play. 'William Lobb' is a Moss rose, with large, loose purplish flowers. I am sure Barrie named his character after it.

At the top of the experts' list is '**Mme Isaac Pereire**'. She is a Bourbon. Let us meet her. She began life in 1881 (so oddly enough did my mother). Her colour is a purplish crimson (so oddly enough . . .). Her flowers are large, fully double and quartered, produced in clusters and singly in the summer and again in a later flush. The flowers are really very large indeed, a good 4 inches

(10cm) across, and she has been regarded as one of the most strongly scented of all roses. Brigadier C. E. Lucas Phillips, in his great book *Ornamental Shrubs* (Cassell, 1981), describes her thus: 'Enormous purple-crimson flowers, voluptuously scented of loose formation. Very vigorous and best used as a pillar rose.' She is so vigorous that she can cover a house wall to the eaves. When well grown on good deep soil she has no peer.

'**Mme Pierre Oger**' was choice number four. She is another Bourbon rose, first introduced in 1878. She has a translucent pink cupped flower of ethereal beauty, and blooms over a long period. The flowers come in clusters of five or six, and have a fine scent.

I can understand Jack Harkness's enthusiasm for '**Mrs John Laing**' (the committee's equal fourth choice), which he calls the most lovely of pink roses. It is a vigorous Hybrid Perpetual first introduced in 1887; it grows to 6 feet (1.8m). The flowers are very large and cupped, and it has an unusual and additional joy for me because the petals all stand out from each other individually, so that you can look into the shadows—lavender shadows—of each petal, and it seems to exude its strong scent from between each of these petals. It is free-flowering and recurrent; the stems are stout and excellent for cutting. The foliage is light green and matt, and it has a very strong constitution. What more could one want of a rose—and that no doubt is why it has remained in the public's favour since 1887, nearly a hundred scented years.

'**Ferdinand Pichard**' was sixth, another Hybrid Perpetual. With 'Rosa Mundi' this is the most effective of the striped roses— the flowers are striped and splashed crimson on a pink ground. They fade to a pale blush pink with age, almost white, while the streaking deepens. He sounds to me a little like an elderly actress! Because he is more double I prefer him to 'Rosa Mundi'. The blooms seem more spectacular. The flowers grow in clusters; they are medium-sized, with a fair scent. Flowering is recurrent. 4 × 4 feet (1.2 × 1.2m) is the size of bush most mentioned; some like it as a hedge.

Why did that most beautiful rose 'Empereur du Maroc', yet another Hybrid Perpetual, only get one vote? (Incidentally, I played the Emperor of Morocco in Dick Whittington—the first television pantomime in 1938—but that is not why I am partial to him.) Flowering is recurrent, and he is seldom over 4 feet (1.2m), for he is not very vigorous. But the flowers are double, deep crimson with shadows of deep maroon. He suffers from what I call a haphazard quartering, but there is enough in the double depths of these blooms for you to bury your nose in the luxuriant velvet and enjoy to the full the deeply scented soul of the rose. I will not be without one. There must be something special about a rose which has been available since 1858 though it is not particularly vigorous. One vote indeed!

'**Boule de Neige**' and '**La Reine Victoria**' were both awarded ten votes. 'Boule de Neige' is a moderately fragrant Bourbon, up to 6 feet (1.8m) tall and the tiniest bit difficult to grow, as it is subject to frosts and it needs a rich soil to give of its best. In a way the flower is like a creamy white camellia—but sometimes the flower becomes too full and ends up like a ball, loose and untidy. However, I've never grown one so I'll shut up about it.

'Ferdinand Pichard', an attractive striped Hybrid Perpetual, and the experts' sixth choice.

'**La Reine Victoria**' is a Bourbon rose, and she's my idea of a perfect Victorian rose. Like that busy little lady herself (all those children and all those letters!), she never stops blooming. The double, globular flowers come in charming clusters of three or four, with the same shell-like petals as her daughter 'Mme Pierre Oger'; she is very much a deeper pink version. Is there another rose of such feminine, delicate charm?

While with the Royals let's look at 'Prince Charles', another Bourbon introduced in 1842. With dark purplish crimson double flowers, he is unlike the other dark red roses in not having a lot of scent, and he is not recurrent either. No wonder nobody voted for him! He is not to be confused with the Scotch (Spinosissima hybrid) double yellow rose called 'Prince Charlie's Rose', introduced in 1828 and also known as 'Old Yellow Scotch'.

'**Kathleen Harrop**' gained nine points. She is a paler pink sport from 'Zéphirine Drouhin', with shell-pink flowers, borne freely for the whole season. She is very subject to mildew, however, and not quite so fragrant as Mum! It will make a good hedge if given the support of wires between posts, as will the parent—I have seen them grown alternately down a long drive to great effect, although the paler rose is not so vigorous.

Three roses tied for tenth place, all with eight points. First is the Hybrid Perpetual '**Baron Girod de l'Ain**'. It is a rich dark crimson-red, maturing to a deep purplish crimson, with a most attractive white edge round the petals, a little like a picotee pink. The petals have dainty fluted edges, reflexed, and the scent is as rich and dark as the colour. It is vigorous, recurrent in flower, and will grow to 5 feet (1.5m). I shall certainly not be able to do without this rose. 'Roger Lambelin' also has dark red petals marked with a narrow white border, similar to a carnation.

Then there is '**Louise Odier**', a Bourbon. This is a warm pink rose with a hint of lavender; it flowers the whole summer through. Another Bourbon, '**Souvenir de la Malmaison**', was also awarded eight points. This is a rose of soft flesh-pink fading to creamy white. It has rightly been called 'Queen of Beauty and Fragrance'; it has been reigning since 1843. The flowers are large—5–6 inches (12.5–15cm) across— very full, opening flat and quartered. Some roses I have described as cup-shaped—this one is a deep saucer of delicate, creamy blush pink. It was named in memory of the rose gardens of the Empress Josephine. The experts say its beauty is unparalleled.

Twelve good recommendations from a wise committee—giving a splendid example of the way the Royal National Rose Society helps the enthusiastic amateur rose grower. Being able, as a member, to receive such excellent advice gives the novice the confidence to grow roses which he had perhaps only caught a glimpse of in some stately home, or seen some brief reference to in a newspaper article, or even heard mention of in a radio phone-in.

One other thing I think the symposium proves—and that is that all our olfactory organs are attuned differently. One expert thinks a rose has a strong scent, another thinks the same rose has hardly any scent at all. Just as we all taste things differently—some like sugar with their tea, some don't—so I think we all have different degrees of smelling the different grades and depths and constituents of perfume. I'm sure we all see different colours differently too. To some sights and sounds and scents exite; to others feeling and words are everything. E. A. Bowles said that phloxes smelt of a 'combination of pepper and pig sties'. Not to me: to me they have a very delicate floriferous smell which reminds me of a tiny garden belonging to my grandfather at Watford, and of hot, sweetly smelling summers. Gertrude Jekyll said she thought that *Lilium pyrenaicum* smelt of mangy dog. Both these opinions prove my point I think.
smelt of mangy dog. Both these opinions prove my point I think.

The Synstylae roses (of which the Musk rose is one) have small, single, creamy white flowers and are of rambling growth. They make up in quantity of flower what they lack in size: having raised themselves to the top of their host shrub or tree, they flower very freely. Their little bunch of styles is united with a column, and the yellow stamens surrounding this column produce the fragrance. *R. filipes* 'Kiftsgate' is a splendid example. It is usual in roses for the petals to exude the fragrance. Here the fragrance is given off freely into the surrounding air; on a still evening in the garden one is surrounded by it; it is an 'experience' every summer. The Sweet briar scents the air, especially after rain, and I contrive always, no matter where I live, to have a bush at every entrance and exit, so that one can brush against it and get the full benefit.

The Incense rose, *R. primula*, has aromatic foliage too. The plant comes from northern China and has buttercup-sized primrose-yellow flowers. That great rosarian S. M. Gault said that the scent reminded him of a heavily laden beehive on a hot day! And Humphrey Brooke of Lime Kiln Gardens thinks that the matchless white flower of the Victorian Perpetual 'Baronne Adolphe de Rothschild' has a scent like cucumber sandwiches!

Likewise the flowers of many old garden roses are fast of their smells while from others the perfume floats in the air. Because the breath of flowers is far sweeter in the air (whence it comes and goes, like the warbling of music), than in the hand, therefore nothing is more fit for delight than to know what be the flowers and plants that do best perfume the air. Roses, damask and red, are fast flowers of their smells; so that you may walk past a whole row of them and find nothing of their sweetness.

FRANCIS BACON, 'OF GARDENS', 1625

7

Breeding a New Rose

Breeding a new rose, we are told, is easy enough for an amateur, but what is difficult—and indeed is surely a matter of chance—is to breed a rose which is different from any existing rose, or, if it is similar to an existing rose, is an improvement on it. Once you have your interesting new progeny in front of you, its qualities have to be proved over several years of trial. But the excitement of the long odds and the chance of a winner are enough to keep the amateur trying—while the superior knowledge of the professional breeder does not seem to shorten the odds very much. Though it is helpful to know what is likely to succeed, the vagaries of nature and her endless vicissitudes still make matters very chancy—which possibly accounts for the try, try, try again happy search of both amateur and professional.

Choosing the parents

With so many hundreds and thousands of named varieties of almost every shade one might well wonder what the present search is for. What is of prime importance is the search for health: we need robust, healthy roses to withstand the scourge of such diseases as blackspot and mildew. So obviously one chooses only strong, healthy parents. Other aspirations are for a dark red rose that does not get mildew, a yellow that does not fade or show traces of pink after the sun has shone strongly on it for days, a white rose that is good after rain and does not 'ball'—and, of course, the complete novelty, such as the first bi-colour rose must have been. Great care goes into the selection of parents by the professional, and thousands and thousands of seedlings are raised (and this, in heated houses and with intensive labour, is a costly procedure). A lot of skill and experience is then needed to detect the desirable characteristics in the new seedlings at an early age.

Right: The 'Cyril Fletcher' rose, raised by Bees of Chester. Its perfume is almost like orange blossom and rose scent combined.

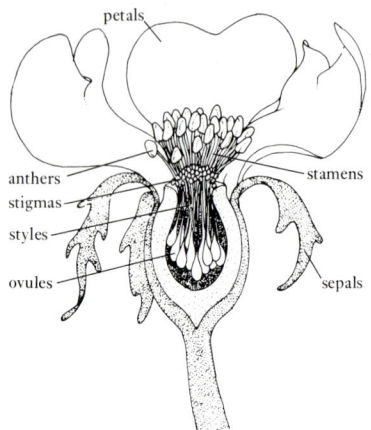

petals
anthers
stigmas
styles
ovules
stamens
sepals

A section of a single rose.

One aspect of knowledge is of the utmost importance to the would-be rose breeder, and that is knowledge of the family tree of the parents you intend to use—and presumably it is because of certain trends and qualities contained in the family tree that you decide upon a particular union. To help you acquire this knowledge there is a book called *Modern Roses 8*—a *Debretts Peerage* of roses combined with a *Who's Who* of roses (published by the McFarland Company, Harrisburg, Pennsylvania, USA). This is the rose breeder's Bible—or the Jockey Club's *Stud Book*, if I may be permitted to mention both books on the same line!

Now let's get slightly technical and tell you that you need to know Mendel's theory. You need to know the chromosome count of the varieties you are to use. The chromosomes are the constituents . . . no we will not get 'slightly' technical, but what I have done I hope without boring you is to point out how very technical a process the breeding of a new rose is, indeed what a miracle a new rose is— because these days a new rose is not just an attractive piece of merchandising; it is, indeed it has to be, an advance in growing a strong, disease-resistant rose to appeal to a more and more discerning public.

In the 1980 *Rose Annual* Jack Harkness, in an article which originally appeared in *The American Rose Annual* of 1979, tells a tale called 'Dreams come true—Almost!'. He describes how he tried to bring the healthy robustness of the 'Rudolph Trimm' rose into brightly coloured Floribundas. After 12,000 experiments the result was one white shrub rose, one white Floribunda of Hybrid Tea type and one green rose. He concludes: 'The stuff that dreams are made of is, therefore, quite clearly different from the end product! But this series of dreams is not ended. "Margaret Merril" and "Green-sleeves" and their descendants are beckoning me treacherously into fresh waters. And I, like a fool, am paddling after them, most likely in the wrong direction.' From this characteristic paragraph one also

THE STAGES OF MY BIRTH

1   Here we see the emasculation of the rose bloom, i.e. the removal of the anthers.

2   The pollen is now being picked up by a camel-hair brush ready to be put on the stigmas of the bride.

3   The pollen being placed on the stigmas.

sees that rose breeding breeds fine breeders. If you will be kind enough to sort that out! To read Jack Harkness's recent book *Roses* (Dent, 1978) is a must.

The method

Having decided on the parents, here is the method. You pot up the selected parents in the autumn in 10-inch (25cm) clay pots or a greenhouse border—obviously using good, strong, healthy plants. One of these plants will be as it were the female—that is to say, the one whose seed will be fertilized by the pollen of the other rose, the male. These you take into the church (sorry the greenhouse—the cold greenhouse) in February.

In the encouraging shelter of the greenhouse the roses will begin to bud and flower by late May—certainly a month in advance of roses outside. You now prepare the rose which is to provide the seed—the bride one might say. Choose a good half-open flower and remove the petals. Next pick off all the anthers and enshrine the poor thing in a paper bag. Do not use a plastic bag: it will not be porous and is inclined to encourage mould. Putting the bride's head in a bag is, I understand, purely optional where there is no risk of cross-pollination from interfering insects.

Next day you go to the other rose, the groom, and pull off all his petals too (the horror of having possibly immortal offspring!). You also cut him from the plant and take him to his bride. Brush his anthers against the stigmas of the bride and replace the paper bag over her head. (At Bees the anthers are stored for twenty-four hours to ensure that the pollen has been shed in sufficient quantity to be applied by camel-hair brush to the stigmas.) You now cherish the bride and either sell off the husband to a supermarket or plant him outside again. But it is terribly important that you, the parson, should fill in the register of the birth, i.e. make very sure you have labelled the wife with her husband's name.

4 Here are the developing heps, to show that the union has been blessed.

5 The seed from the ripened heps has now been sown, and here are the germinating seedlings.

6 The seedlings in flower.

Here I am in the greenhouse at Bees, watching Tony Hallows choosing possible future roses for eventual fame.

After a couple of weeks or so you can take off the paper bag. By the autumn this parent bush will have nicely swollen seed-heads which you cull when ripe and shiny. Plant them in a peaty mixture in a flower pot, covering with wire mesh to keep out mice, and put them outside for the frost to stratify—or you can use a refrigerator as the professionals do. In February—a year from commencement you note—you bring the hips indoors and squeeze the seeds from the hips over a bowl of water. Some of the seeds will float and some will sink: the sinkers are the ones we need. Sow them in seed compost, and when the seedlings have produced a few leaves other than the original two, pot them off separately into small pots. Some people simply sow the whole lot. Germination will in any case be erratic.

When the seedling has grown to 4 inches (10cm) or so it will produce its first flower. Sometimes this is a single, even though the eventual flowers will be double, so disregard the first one—indeed, if I was not an impatient man I'd pinch out the first bloom to strengthen the little bush for further flowering.

The excitement is now mounting. Some of these seedlings will be sufficiently mature to produce more flowers in June. This is when you take your pick. I beg of you do not throw away the winner! Of course, the professional breeder will pick out the good characteristics with more certainty than the amateur. The good ones you will grow on, and you will have bred your own rose—next year you can plant it out in the garden and call the neighbours round to admire.

THE CYRIL FLETCHER ROSE
Now at the Chelsea Flower Show of 1981 I was asked by Mr Terry Kenwright, Managing Director of Bees, if I would like to have a rose named after me. I was so pleased and so thrilled that I had to mask my enthusiasm with suitable humility. Here, I said to myself, as I accepted, was my immortality! 'We have several promising new seedlings,' he said. 'You must come to Chester later in the summer

and select the one you would like to bear your name.' I have frequently said that I think a rose without a strong scent is not a rose at all, so in the train on my way to Sealand, Chester, I kept saying to myself, 'It must smell!' I may in my enthusiasm have spoken out loud, because I arrived in an empty carriage. It had slowly emptied!

I had never actually been in a field of roses before. Acres of blooming roses stretched before and around me. The scent was glorious, and the rows and rows of familiar and not so familiar roses made a delightful picture. If you have never been to one of the great rose nurseries, then you really must do so. The fields at Sealand are flat and open; it is reclaimed land from the sea as the name suggests. With an open summer sky and a blazing sun it was beautiful, but with winter's steely blast I could imagine it must have been a pretty bleak place—ideal for the growing of hardy plants.

In my mind I had visualized the ultimate in dark red roses, but the new bushes did not contain a dark red. There was a very attractive pink, but the one which took all my attention was a white rose with a yellowy, creamy, greenish tinge towards its heart. It had a strong, arresting perfume. Almost like orange blossom and rose combined. 'This has an odd odour,' I exclaimed, and they laughed. 'Obviously the right rose for you,' they said, and I agreed. I had chosen me. It was a blissful moment for me to know that this flower of great beauty was to bear my name. Sad for the rose that a dilapidated comedian with a love of roses should give his name to it. Its picture is at the beggining of this chapter, and I'm sure you will agree with me that it is the most beautiful rose. I am honoured that it has my name, but the creators of this beautiful flower should be the ones to honour.

Budding

As we have seen, you cannot propagate roses from seed with any certainty of knowing how your seeds will turn out. You can propagate roses by cuttings, but these take a long time to grow into a bush (three years approximately!), and the Hybrid Teas are often difficult. What is needed is a vigorous rootstock, to speed the cutting along as it were. And also, in the instance of a new rose, to propagate from the parent bush as many roses as possible. This is done by cutting a 'bud' from the parent—a tiny, dormant leaf-axil bud—and grafting it on to a vigorous type of rootstock. The nurseryman uses *R. canina*, *R. multiflora*, *R. rugosa* or 'Laxa', which is mostly sucker-free.

Select a strong shoot of bud-wood, with three or four buds. Strip off the leaves, leaving short pieces of stalk where the buds are lying in the axils. Now make a T-shaped cut in the bark at the base of the rootstock, just above the roots. The stem of the T should be about 1 inch (2.5cm) long. Cut an oval of bud-wood from the shoot, with the bud in the middle of it, remove the wood from behind the bud, and insert it in the T-shaped cut. The bud then rests against the white wood of the rootstock, enclosed by its bark. Bind firmly with raffia. Do this between late June and August, and by the following spring it should have 'taken'. Now cut off the top-growth of the rootstock just above the budding union. Practise the exercise—best of all watch a professional doing it. A good budder can do 5,000 a day.

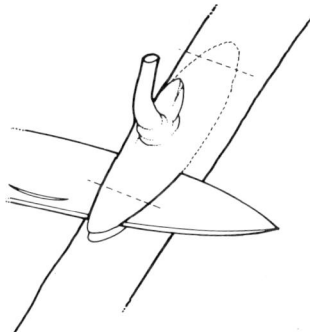

First the bud with an oval sliver of bark is cut from the rose stalk. Any wood behind the bud will have to be removed.

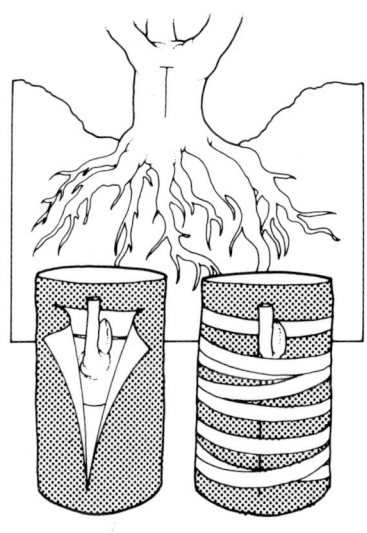

A T-shaped slit is cut in the rootstock. The sides of the slit are rolled back and the bud of the cultivar is inserted. The slit is then tied up firmly with raffia.

8

Planning a Rose Garden

So we want a garden of roses to cherish through our summer-dazzled days. If our garden is big enough we can have a separate area devoted entirely to roses, and if we are only blessed with a small plot we will have our shrub roses in our mixed shrub and herbaceous border, and our Hybrid Teas in a single bed, with rambler and climbing roses all over the fences and all over the house. If we have a front garden and a back garden which is too small to cut into two, why not devote either the front or the back garden entirely to roses? You could perhaps plant bulbs to brighten the spring, and have some ground cover plants under the roses, as I have suggested in Chapter 4.

If you have a large garden then a splendid expedient of design is to turn various parts of the garden into separate outdoor 'rooms', and one of these can be the rose garden. Different levels, existing hedges or walls (yew hedges, or ancient brick or stone walls, we hope), large trees, belts of shrubbery or woodland, perhaps a pond or a stream— all these features in a garden lend themselves to helping to form separate shapes or enclosures. Paths do too; so do loggias and summerhouses; even the overhanging eaves of the zoo next door can be useful!

But whatever you do with roses in your garden, think as largely as possible. Plant with an eye to the flamboyance of the future. Roses are exotic plants; they are the distillation of high summer in the garden. In a drab world they are an extravagance in scent and colour, a benison for the tired mind. Make your rose gardens glamorous— do things here which will be bewitchingly exaggerated and theatrical. Over-plant, have too many roses, use every device to exploit them: arbours, trellis, walls, old garden ornaments. Garland hideous old trees with roses, even have them in hanging baskets and window boxes.

Right: A luxuriant entrance for a garden, using climbing roses in profusion. You could achieve this effect in a large or small garden.

AN AVERAGE SIZE ROSE GARDEN

How are we to achieve this horticultural flamboyance? Let us look at plan 1, which is a suggestion for a garden 100 feet by 45 feet (30 × 13.5m)—a little larger than the tiny plot most new houses have.

The house is fronted by a terrace 10 feet (3m) wide. There will be pockets of soil near the house to accommodate the roses that will cover the house. I suggest we use 'Mme Alfred Carrière' in Bed A, a white rose, recurrent and strongly scented, which will climb 20 feet (6m). Below her, to cover the bottom part of the wall should she get leggy, we will have 'Penelope', salmon-apricot pink and recurrent, a vigorous Hybrid Musk rose growing to 10 feet (3m). In bed B let us have 'Climbing Cécile Brunner', a vigorous rose which will cover up to 20 feet (6m). She has small, double, blush pink flowers, in sprays, and is recurrent. In front, should she get leggy, and as a nice contrast, the blousy yellow roses of 'Golden Showers' will enchant with continuous bloom the whole summer through. In both beds, to stretch out on to the stones of the terrace, we will have Sam McGredy's new rose 'Snow Carpet', which does not mind if you tread on it. Here in two beds I have explained my policy of exuberance—three roses when one would have done!

Along the front of the terrace we will have narrow borders of miniature roses, and in bed X against the fence we will have 'Laneii' (Lane's Moss), which grows to 5 feet (1.5m) and has mauvish crimson flowers of moss type; it flowers in June but is also recurrent. In Y opposite we will use a vigorous Rugosa, 'Roseraie de l'Hay', with large purple-maroon flowers, decorative heps in autumn, and yellow autumnal foliage. It grows up to 8 feet (2.4m) tall.

At the opposite end of the garden we will have an arbour with a seat in it, and this will be covered with two roses. *R. filipes* 'Kiftsgate' will cover it in no time at all. It flowers memorably once a season, in June, and has tiny white flowers in enormous clusters which will scent a whole suburb. The other rose has no scent at all but single flowers of crimson which have a curiously long life; it is called 'Parkdirektor Riggers' and will flower from June till October.

Beds C and D will contain closely planted bushes of 'Iceberg', a Floribunda rose. This, as the name suggests, is white, semi-double with a slight fragrance; it is a vigorous rose which goes on and on. There are also two standard roses in each bed, and these are to be of 'Blue Moon'. The colour is silvery lilac, and it has large blooms which do not have a very strong stem and will therefore be seen to advantage as a standard. It has a strong lemon/rose perfume, and the delicate colour will be much set off by the white 'Icebergs'.

Beds E and F will both be bedded closely with 'Margaret Merril', a pearly white, with a hint of the palest shell-pink salmon, with standard roses of 'Chanelle', which is buff, peach, pink and cream, a vigorous grower with abundant flowers. Beds G and H will be bedded out with 'Troika'. The colour is one of those bronzy blends so popular in the 1970s. The next two beds will contain the 'Cyril Fletcher' rose, a greenish white, tallish with a good strong fragrance. This is planted here to stop the bold pink of 'Prima Ballerina' used in

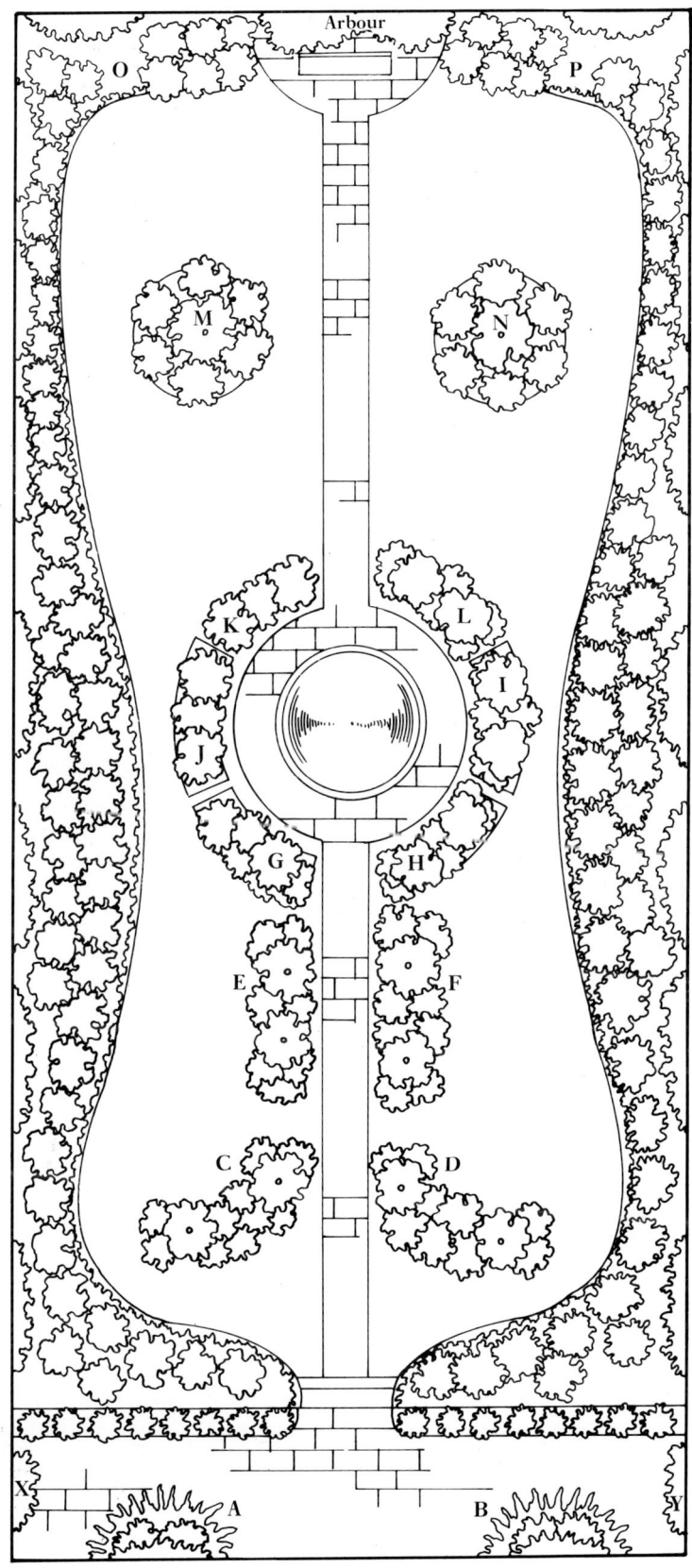

Plan 1: An average size
garden, 100 × 45 feet
(30 × 13.5m). The beds will be
planted out as follows:
A: 'Mme Alfred Carrière',
'Penelope' and 'Snow Carpet'.
B: 'Climbing Cécile Brunner',
'Golden Showers'
and 'Snow Carpet'.
X: 'Laneii'.
Y: 'Roseraie de l'Hay'.
C & D: 'Iceberg' and two
standard 'Blue Moon'.
E & F: 'Margaret Merril' and
two standard 'Chanelle'.
G & H: 'Troika'.
J & L: 'Cyril Fletcher'.
K & L: 'Prima Ballerina'.
M & N: 'Josephine Bruce' and
'Mme Louis Laperrière'.
O & P: 'Grandpa Dixon' and
'King's Ransom'.
Over the arbour will be *R.
filipes* 'Kiftsgate' and
'Parkdirektor Riggers'. There
will be shrub roses in the long
borders and climbers
and ramblers on the walls.

Beds K and L from clashing with the bronzy vermilion of 'Troika'. It can be very helpful to use a white or cream rose in this way in a small area where strongly coloured plants might otherwise clash.

On either side of the arbour, in areas O and P, we will have yellow roses: half a dozen of 'Grandpa Dixon' on one side and another half dozen of 'King's Ransom' on the other. These will form a good light background to the deep maroon shades of beds M and N, which will contain 'Josephine Bruce' and 'Mme Louis Laperrière'. In the centre of each of these beds we will have a standard rose of 'Ernest H. Morse', giving us the strong lighter crimson which at the moment we lack.

On either side of the grass, as a border between the grass and the fence, will be an assortment of shrub roses, including amongst the older varieties the 'modern old-fashioned shrub roses' 'Nevada' (a single, pale creamy white) and 'Constance Spry', with large, blousy, heavily fragrant blooms of a Victorian pink. The climbers at the back will include 'Dr W. van Fleet' (blush white), 'Zéphirine Drouhin' (pink), 'Allen Chandler' (a deep velvety crimson, with very large flowers), 'Climbing Lady Hillingdon' (apricot), 'Mermaid' (a single, large yellow with lovely glistening dark green foliage), *R. banksiae lutea* (a double yellow primrose-type rose, very early) on one side; and on the other 'Canary Bird' (a single primrose-type rose, very early in April and with fernlike foliage), 'Albertine' (the popular pink rambler with a touch of salmon in its semi-double flowers), and 'Veilchenblau', a glorious violet-purple but not recurrent-flowering.

All these roses will be a mass of bloom, scent and colour, all in an area 100 feet by 45 feet (30 × 13.5m), either as a separate part of a garden or as a garden on its own. If this is to be a garden on its own then some clematis planted amongst the climbers will help out with blue and some ground cover plants should be used amongst the Hybrid Teas and Floribundas. Pale blue pansies could be used in beds C and D, apricot pansies and an edging of Santolina for beds E and F. Beds G and H could be underplanted with *Ajuga reptans*, and J and I with *Convolvulus Cneorum*. You could use purple sage in K and L, with pale pink petunias in M and N. You will have ample scope for clumps of herbaceous plants, irises, etc., amongst the shrub rose borders—but all of this supposes that the plan here envisaged is the whole garden.

However, even if this rose garden is a garden amongst others, full use should be made of spring bulbs. It is an exercise of fun and ingenuity to try and choose tulips of different species and kinds and shapes to match, or almost match, the colours of the roses to come. This is a small example of the extra fun one can always find in a garden. Another idea might be to get some old copies of *Country Life* (what a joy it is to have a beautifully produced magazine *each week*, which keeps up its standards of printing and reproduction, to say nothing of the content which from a gardening point of view is always first class), find some garden view of Edwardian or even Victorian flavour, and try to copy it—or at least repeat some period feature in it that will then lend a new dimension and flavour to your own garden.

A VERY SMALL GARDEN

Looking at Plan 2 we see a very small garden, 10 feet by 12 feet (3 × 3.6m), almost square. It could well be a front garden. We have made the centre bed the feature. This will house perhaps ten Hybrid Teas or Floribundas. Whatever roses you decide on, one important thing to remember is to get a uniformity of height and habit in this centre bed, as it is so small. Different heights bobbing up here and there would look very ragged.

On the house we will grow our usual climbing rose, with a tall shrub rose in front to furnish the bottom reaches with bloom, and perhaps a clematis or wisteria as well. On the side walls of fences use climbing and rambler or pillar roses and then, as this is the only garden the house has, use other shrubs (evergreens preferably) for winter furnishing, and herbaceous plants and bulbs. Lilies go especially well with roses, and use Darwin or parrot tulips for the centre bed in spring. The paving can be of York stone or simulated stone. In the centre of the bed you could have a sundial or bird bath or, of course, a standard rose. A standard rose could also be used at each corner. Instead of the hedge round the centre bed you could have a hedge of miniature roses (all of one colour to give it uniformity—and of course that colour must blend with the roses in the bed).

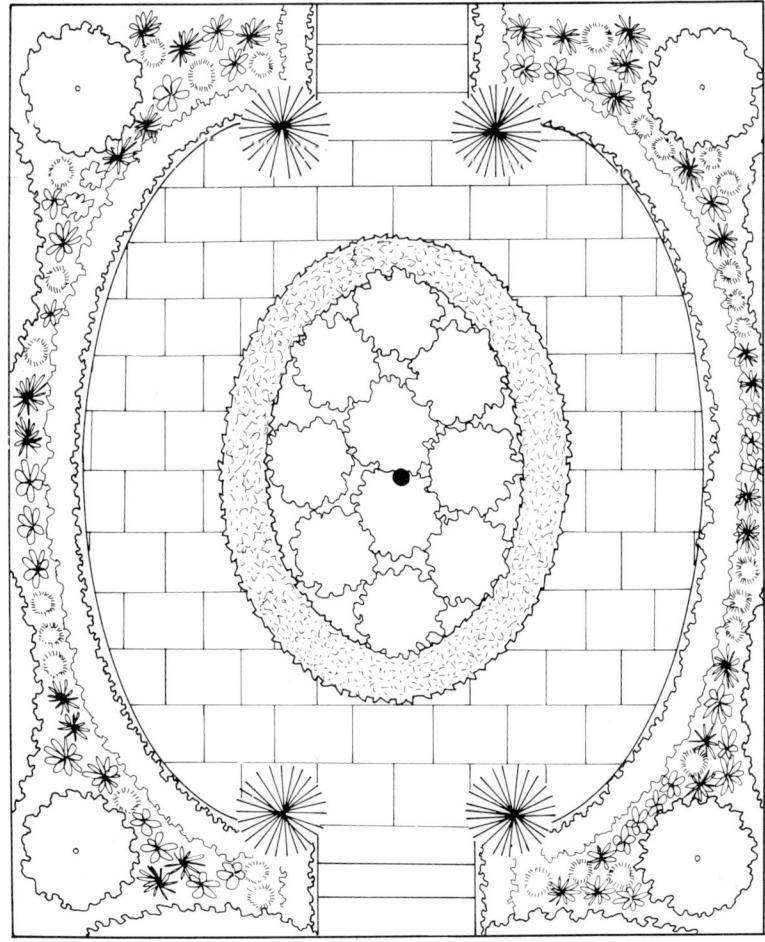

Plan 2: A small garden 10 × 12 feet (3 × 3.6m). The centre bed will house perhaps ten Hybrid Teas or Floribundas. You could decide on one repeat-flowering variety; you could have a selection of yellow, cream and white roses; you could decide on a collection of the present popular bronzy, apricot to vermilion shades, or you could get a 'Fragrant Collection' from a rose breeder. Climbers, ramblers and pillar roses will clothe the walls of the house and the side walls or fences.

A LARGE SEPARATE ROSE GARDEN

Plan 3 is for a large separate rose garden. I have imagined that we are going to use a very large walled kitchen garden, so we will have lovely mature surrounding walls of either stone or brick. If the walls are of brick then the pillars of the pergola must be made of brick too, and the elevated sides of the pond. I have raised the level of the water here to about 3 feet (90cm). The roses planted around it will be perhaps $2\frac{1}{2}$ feet (75cm) or so, and so will not obscure the surface of the water—which will reflect the joyous sun-kissed faces of the roses on the pergola roof looking down. The paths I would like (in my opulent fashion) to be York stone slabs. Or they could be brick, in herringbone pattern—old bricks please.

The farthest vista—although this is not a garden of vistas—is a semi-circular yew hedge in front of which is a white marble statue of considerable presence. The pond will have no statue—just a single rose jet of water, rising from the surface as if by magic.

All round the garden, growing against the walls, will be climbers and ramblers of all kinds and colours, varieties and species, and in the borders will be dozens of shrub roses, old and new. They will contrast with each other according to season, with grey foliage and red foliage as well as all the colours of the blooms from deepest mauve through dark red and pink to shell-pink, beige, pale yellow and white.

Immediately on entering there is a multiplicity of geometrical beds cut out of the lawns. A, B, C and D will each be planted with one variety of Hybrid Tea or Floribunda rose, and these beds will all be edged with Santolina to give a uniform appearance. Beds E, F, G, H and I are all bedded out with tiny miniature roses, as in an old parterre garden. Mr Tony Gregory tells me this is possible, and will be happy to plant a garden like this to my design one day—but not unfortunately in time for this book. Beds J, K, L and M will be planted out with roses of subtly graded colours, as I suggest in Chapter 9 when talking about Queen Mary's Rose Garden, Regent's Park (p. 95). O, P, Q, R, S and T are again beds for Hybrid Tea and Floribunda roses, to be chosen by the owner. I suggest some of the oldest, tried and true friends, and some of the very newest. The pergola has fifty pillars for climbing and pillar roses, and I would like a veritable canopy of roses, of every colour and every kind—even vigorous roses like 'Seagull' and *R. filipes* 'Kiftsgate' may be used. A flamboyance indeed!

There will be hundreds of roses here in this enclosure of old walls, and the air in summer will be heavy with their beauty.

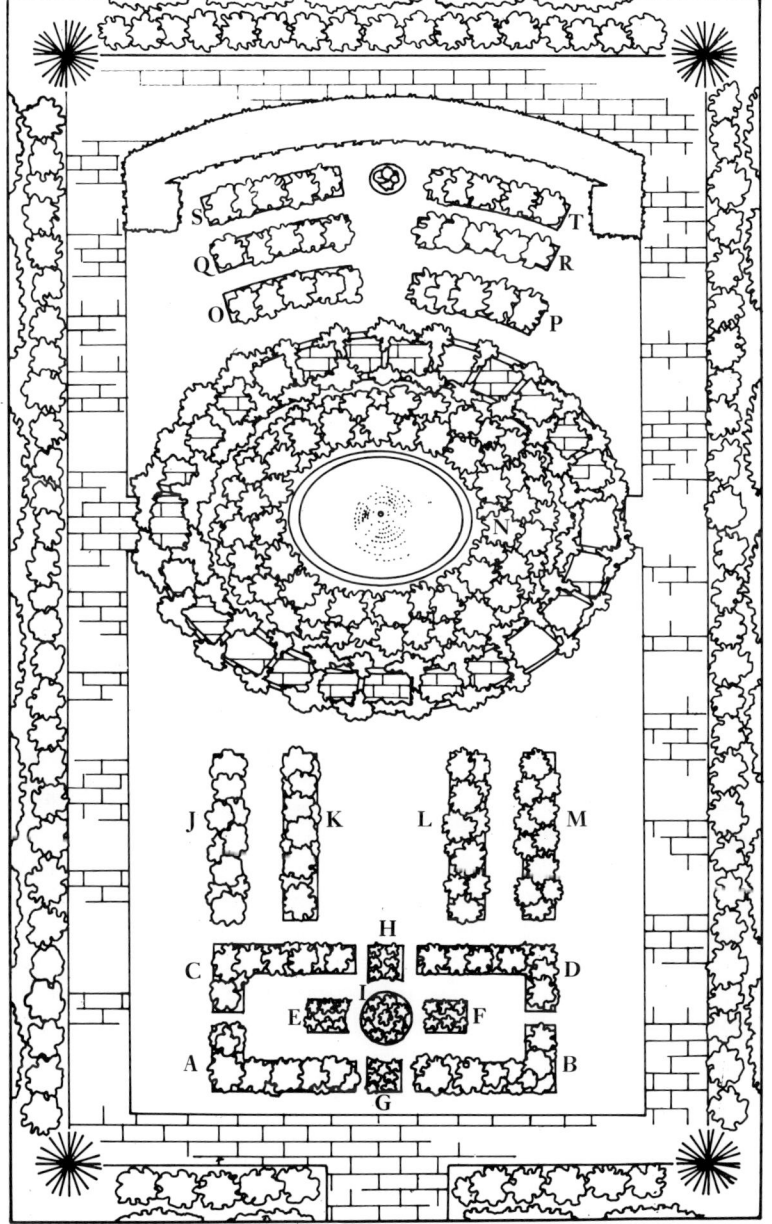

Plan 3: A large separate rose garden, based on a walled kitchen garden.

A, B, C & D will each contain one variety of Hybrid Tea or Floribunda.

E, F, G, H & I: miniatures.

J, K, L & M: roses of subtly graded colours.

O, P, Q, R, S & T: Hybrid Teas and Floribundas.

The pergola has fifty pillars for climbing and pillar roses; climbers and ramblers will grow against the walls, and shrub roses in the borders.

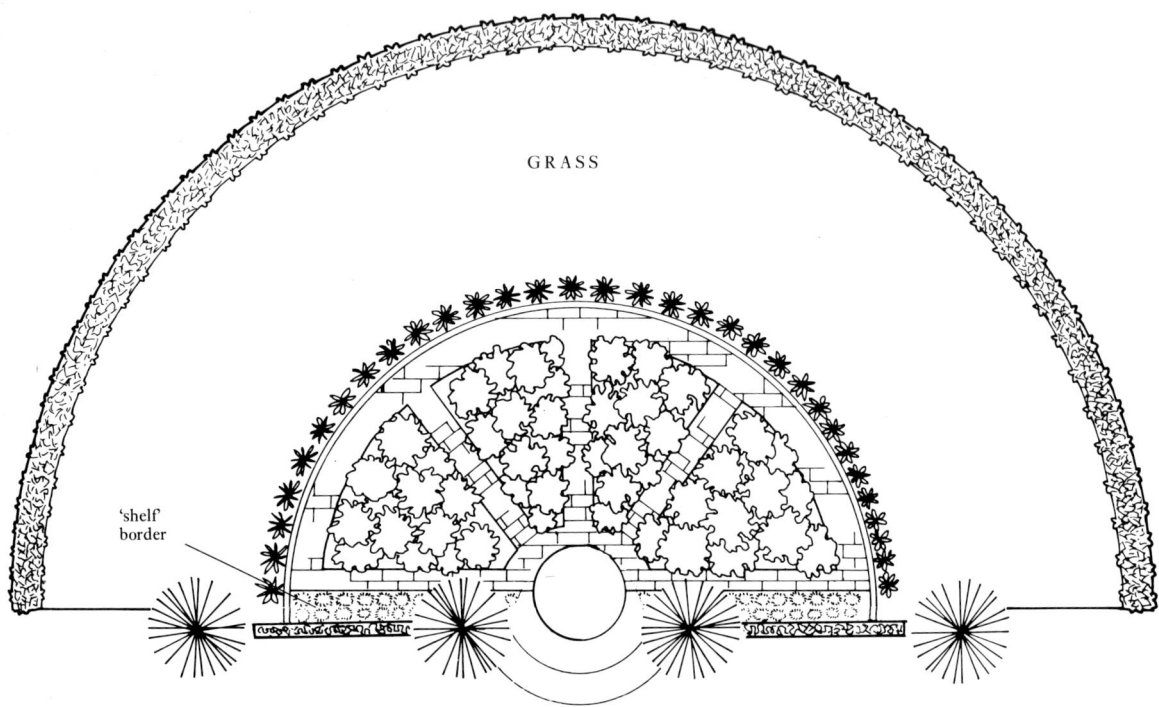

GRASS

'shelf'
border

**Plan 4: Garden for an exposed
site. The lower beds are 2–2½
feet (60–75cm) below ordinary
ground level, and the lavender
hedge gives another foot
(30cm) of protection. The
beds can be planted with
Hybrid Teas and Floribundas,
or with the old shrub roses.**

GARDEN FOR AN EXPOSED SITE

Plan 4 is for a fan-shaped sunken rose garden with a 'shelf' on the
long straight side for herbaceous plants, miniature roses or ground
cover roses, which is intersected by steps based on a stone mill-
wheel if obtainable. This garden plan is especially useful if you have
an exposed site where your roses would get battered by a prevailing
wind (perhaps near the coast). It can be of any size, according to the
site. The depth of the garden can be about 1 foot (30cm) down to the
shelf and then a further foot or 18 inches (30–45cm) down to the
lower bed level. Then if your lavender hedge is about 1 foot (30cm)
high you will be giving the roses 3 feet (90cm) of shelter. A yew or
beech hedge, perhaps 4 feet (1.2m) high, and at least 12 feet (3.6m)
away, will then give you all the shelter you need. It is imperative,
however, that proper drains should be laid so that the whole garden
does not become a lake! These drains must lead away to a sump dug
2 or 3 feet (60–90cm) deeper than the rose garden, with proper
overflows to conduct water away.

I have indicated in the plan the sort of planting envisaged. Hybrid
Teas or Floribundas give a more uniform effect, but with drystone
walls and old brick paths the old shrub roses would love this habitat,
and they would look very much at home.

ANOTHER LARGE SEPARATE ROSE GARDEN

Plan 5 (overleaf) is based on an old Victorian rose garden. Presumably this would have been a separate rose garden, part of a larger garden, but there is nothing to stop you using this plan for your whole garden. In this case I would use beds A and C for herbaceous plants and small shrubs rather than for roses so that there was something of interest in the winter. Similarly I would have a boundary hedge of various flowering and evergreen shrubs.

If this is to be a separate rose garden then I suggest the boundary hedge should be of yew. Beds A, B, C and D will be planted with old shrub roses and the centre beds 1–6 should each be planted with a different variety of Floribunda or Hybrid Tea. Each of these centre beds will contain two standard roses, but not of the same variety as the rest of the bed. The paths shown darkly shaded in the plan can be of old brick (herringbone pattern), York stone paving, simulated stone paving or gravel. I would prefer the York paving or simulated stone, and in the crevices I would plant thyme and similar small plants to enhance the perfume of the whole. At the entrance and exit of the garden I would have topiary yews, with a low-growing hedge of Santolina round the centre circle, box hedges round B and D and Hidcote lavender round A and C.

May I suggest the following plantings, with a special eye to creating a magnificent grouping of colour. All these roses have fragrance; they are all repeat flowering and graded by the nurserymen as of medium height.

'**Prima Ballerina**' A superb pink with large flowers. Hybrid Tea.

'**Korresia**' Yellow flowers borne in sprays of Hybrid Tea type, though this is a Floribunda.

'**Just Joey**' A Hybrid Tea with large blooms of deep copper—very attractive when fully open.

'**Margaret Merril**' A Floribunda-Hybrid Tea type, with creamy white blooms.

'**City of Leeds**' Floribunda with magical bronzy/red/pink foliage when young, amongst which appear wide sprays of shapely, semi-double salmon blooms. It is considered one of the best bedding roses of the present day.

'**News**' A Floribunda of sturdy growth, beetroot-red at the bud stage opening to purple and deepening almost to violet with age. It is very free-flowering over a long period. Its parents are 'Lilac Charm', a Floribunda, and 'Tuscany Superb', which is a Gallica. When I saw a bed of these close-to, I thought what a vulgar magenta colour and walked away. Then I saw its glorious misty purple—a large square bed of it at Bone Hill—from a distance. I thought, what a fabulous colour to use, and went up to the bed again. I looked again at the flat crinkly flowers, some almost ruby-red—well ruby-purple—some really magenta and some mauve (the word mauve is French for mallow, and this explains everything), and began really to like the colour, and certainly the robust habit of the plant itself. Then I thought, what a challenge to place in a rose garden. I thought, it will go well with pink, with a salmony colour on the other side. Magenta and salmon are wonderfully good together as 'intentional clashes'.

Now what about the standards, two of the same colour for each bed—and we must think not only of the colour of the roses in the beds beneath the standards; we have to think of the neighbouring standards as well. To go with 'Prima Ballerina' I have chosen two standards of 'Josephine Bruce', and with 'Korresia' two standards of 'Wendy Cussons'. For 'Just Joey' we will have two standard 'Blue Moon'; for 'Margaret Merril' I have chosen—a subtle combination here—two standards of the golden amber 'Whisky Mac'. For 'City of Leeds' let us have two standards of 'King's Ransom' (yellow), and for 'News' two standards of the Floribunda 'Iced Ginger'. 'Iced Ginger' was exhibited at the Chelsea Flower Show in 1982, and it caught my attention even though it was surrounded by so much other beauty. It is a bi-colour with shapely blooms of cream, shaded a gingery pink. It may be difficult to get as a standard, but as it carries its flowers in large sprays it will look very splendid over 'News'. I like these two kinds of colours together. One of my most successful flower arrangements, which I often repeat, is a rose bowl of 'Whisky Mac' roses and the darkest possible purple sweet peas. (And the scent!)

What plants do we choose for ground cover under these exotic plantings? I think it would be unnecessarily fidgety to choose a different ground cover for each bed, and we would detract from all these carefully chosen colours. I would like one plant for the whole circle, and the plant I have chosen is *Ophiopogon planiscarpus nigrescens*. This is an extremely unusual plant, one of the few black-leaved plants in existence, with purple-black foliage and black berries. It's like a black, slowly creeping, strap-like grass 6 inches (15cm) high. X represents a statue or a sundial in the centre of the roundel.

Beds A, B, C and D must all contain the old shrub roses, the shortest ones near the path and the taller ones near the yew hedges. I do not mind you using an occasional Floribunda group such as 'Iceberg' or 'Ballerina' in the foreground if you are out of suitable colours, but they must look like shrub roses. And I will allow you to grow lilies amongst them to continue the spread of flowering time— so arrange them to flower between the June exuberance and the repeat flowering in September.

Having been so definite with our colour schemes with the Hybrid Teas, let us do the same with the shrub roses. We will decide to use Beds A and C for pink and dark pink and dark red roses and Beds B and D for white and yellow. Let us at the same time make sure we use the repeat flowerers as well as the once flowering roses in each bed to give us a good show in September, and let us decide on one good ground cover plant for all four beds. I suggest dwarf evergreen azaleas,endeavouring to purchase and plant only those of the same form and possibly the same colours—white and pink and dark cerise. Or we could use the geranium 'Johnson's Blue'—a fine hybrid with many cup-shaped light blue flowers and a long flowering period (1 foot (30cm) high).

Plan 5: Another large separate
rose garden, this one based on
an old Victorian rose garden.
A, B, C & D: old shrub roses.
1–6: 'Prima Ballerina',
'Korresia', 'Just Joey',
'Margaret Merril',
'City of Leeds' and 'News'.

Pale Pink

'Félicité Parmentier' (Alba) For the front of the border. Compact shrub with flat reflex flowers of a soft pink; highly scented. Flowers once.

'Fantin-Latour' (Centifolia) Pale blush pink, full blooms, opening flatter and paler. Flowers once; 5 feet (1.5m).

'Gruss an Aachen' For front of bed. Flesh-pink changing to cream. Shapely double flowers, fragrant and a deeper pink on the inside. Almost a Hybrid Tea-type bloom. Recurrent.

'La France' Pale pink—the earliest Hybrid Tea. Recurrent; 4 feet (1.2m).

'La Reine Victoria' (Bourbon) Pale lilac-pink and recurrent. Scented. 5–6 feet (1.5–1.8m).

'Old Blush' (Perpetual Chinese) Silvery pink. Scented. 3–4 feet (90cm–1.2m).

Dark Pink

'Constance Spry' Modern shrub rose. Large cabbagy pink blooms with a fine scent. Tallish.

R. californica plena Rich lilac-pink, semi-double flowers. Well scented and needs a lot of space. Usually recurrent.

'Aloha' Double Hybrid Tea-type. Large, strong pink, scented flowers, deep pink in the centre and fading at the edges. Prune to a large shrub. Recurrent.

Maroon and Dark Red

'F. J. Grootendorst' (Rugosa) Bright crimson and recurrent. Small, rather ball-like double flowers. Scentless. 5–8 feet (1.5–2.4m).

'Baron Girod de l'Ain' Hybrid Perpetual. Large, double, bright dark crimson-red flowers, edged with white and maturing to a purplish crimson. Recurrent; 5 feet (1.5m).

'Gloire de Ducher' Hybrid Perpetual. Bright purplish crimson. Large double flowers, well scented. Recurrent; 7 feet (2.1m).

'Capitaine John Ingram' Small, double moss flowers, of a dark crimson purple, rather globular. Non-recurrent; 5 feet (1.5m).

'William Lobb' Dark purple Moss rose. Scented. Non-recurrent; 7 feet (2.1m).

'Great Western' A vigorous Bourbon (seen and admired at Lime Kiln Garden). Large purple-maroon flowers. Flowers once. 5 feet (1.5m).

'Mrs Anthony Waterer' A lovely dark crimson Rugosa. Scented, and recurrent, but with rather a poor crop of autumn flowers. 4 × 7 feet (1.2 × 2.1m).

Far left: 'Golden Showers'
(climber). Left: 'Mrs Anthony
Waterer' (Rugosa). Top:
'Great Western' (Bourbon)
Above left: 'Félicité
Parmentier', an Alba with
highly scented blooms.
Above right: 'Capitaine
John Ingram' (Moss rose).

White

'Souvenir de la Malmaison' A superb Bourbon rose of lovely blush, white with face-powder pink shadings. Each bloom is beautifully proportioned and opens out to a flat quartered shape. Scented. Make sure you buy the bush and not the climber. It flowers mid to late June and again in September, and grows to 4 feet (1.2m). Named after the garden of the Empress Josephine.

'Iceberg' For the front of the bed, a Floribunda with medium-sized, moderately full flowers, borne in clusters. It flowers continuously throughout the summer, and has just enough scent to please me.

R. rugosa alba This is the parent of the great race of Rugosa roses. White, scented, single flowers with lots of golden stamens and pointed buds. Recurrent; 6–7 feet (1.8–2.1m).

R. arvensis Single, creamy white flowers—useful as ground cover. Flowers in June or July.

'Little White Pet' This forms a 2 feet × 2 feet (60cm × 60cm)

'Alchymist', a modern shrub rose, very double yellow, scented, non-recurrent.

bush—supposedly a China rose, with scent and blooms of creamy white all summer.

'Perpetual White Moss' Also known as 'Quatre Saisons Blanc Mousseux'. Fragrant and gloriously mossy! Recurrent; tall.

R. centifolia muscosa alba White, with very mossy buds. Outstandingly strong perfume. Not recurrent. 4 feet (1.2m).

'Gloire Lyonnaise' Hybrid Perpetual, with huge, cupped, very double, scented flowers of pure white with a lemon base. Recurrent. 3 feet × 3 feet (90cm × 90cm).

Yellow roses to mingle with the white

'Agnes' A vigorous hybrid Rugosa. Amber-yellow flowers, fading to cream, 3 inches (7.5cm) across. Very scented and recurrent. 6 feet (1.8m).
'Alchymist' Modern shrub. Very double yellow and scented.

'Golden Moss' A recent moss introduced in 1932. Excellent scent. Not recurrent; 6 feet (1.8m).

'Danae' A Hybrid Musk rose, buff yellow, fading to cream with age. It flowers continuously all summer, and forms a bush 5 × 4 feet (1.5 × 1.2m). I think this rose has a touch of apricot in it, both in colour and scent.

'Old Yellow Scotch' (*Spinosissima*) Small, double, non-fading, golden yellow flowers, borne early on a spiny, compact plant. Not to be confused with 'Whisky Mac'! It has a pleasant perfume. Not recurrent. It was raised in Worcester by a Mr Williams of Pitmaston, famous for his apples and pears. Williams Pear I wonder?

'Francesca' A Hybrid Musk, scented and vigorous. It flowers all summer, with semi-double apricot flowers in large sprays on strong stems. 6 feet (1.8m).

'Golden Showers' With me this never grew higher than 9 feet (2.7m) or so—and it never ceased blooming with loosely double flowers fading to cream. It has a slight fragrance—but not too little for me to banish it!

You would have to have a large garden to be able to have the exuberance of roses I have described. Just choose enough to clothe your plot. I have spent longer choosing the plants for this garden than for the other four put together, and one day I will actually plant it as I have listed it here. I have made corners of it here and there in gardens I have had through the years, but I have never brought everything together in this mouth-watering collage. The absurd thing is that it would not cost a fortune to create all this beauty—just patience and a few pounds. The ground to put it on would, I suppose, be costly today, but the greatest expenditure would be your precious time. The interest on the expenditure, however, would increase every year, rewarding you in a way that Lombard Street never could.

9

Famous Rose Gardens

It is an excellent idea for us to visit some of the famous rose gardens; so here in hand we go to see what we can decide upon for our own gardens by visiting the great.

QUEEN MARY'S ROSE GARDEN, REGENTS PARK
In the twenties the Royal National Rose Society held its Summer Show in the Royal Botanical Gardens at Regents Park, London. When the Royal Botanical Society's lease expired, the various buildings were demolished and the area was absorbed into the rest of Regents Park. In 1932 the British Rose Growers' Association made a gift of rose bushes to Regents Park, and this was followed up by further supplies in following years. Thus was born the circular rose garden known to the Regents Park gardeners as the Cartwheel. It became so outstanding a rose garden that soon King George V welcomed the suggestion that it should be called Queen Mary's Garden, and as such rose-lovers from all over the world have known it.

I visited Queen Mary's Rose Garden in June 1982, and I must say I was a little depressed at the condition of many of the shrub roses. These are vigorous and bold, and not subject to disease as the Hybrid Teas and Floribundas are, but here they were very much the poor relations. How I yearned to get on the phone and order a few loads of old horse manure. The soil was dark and dry and looked like a back garden in London that had had no natural manure for decades. I know it must have done—but the roses were certainly not responding to whatever food they were receiving. And a lot of the name tabs were just not there: I know vandalism is one of our few growing industries and I expect this was the reason. Apart from a lot of mildew on the old roses—the new bedding out ones were spotless and wonderfully healthy—I felt the garden was generally well kept, but replacements for some of the shrub roses were much needed.

Right: A view across beds of massed Hybrid Teas towards the lake at Regents Park. What other flower could be used to such effect?

Top: 'Deep Secret'. Above: 'Lady Johnson'. Right: 'Helen Traubel' (Hybrid Teas). There were beds of all three in Queen Mary's Rose Garden, growing luxuriantly.

It was about 5 o'clock when I was there, and very hot. It should have been a long golden afternoon, but I was not entirely happy. I cheered enormously, however, when I saw a bed of 'Wendy Cussons', closely planted and gloriously in bloom. This rose was first introduced in 1959; the rosy scarlet blooms are full, and the perfume is strong. The bed was also most effectively arranged: along the back were very strongly flowering standards at regular intervals, and in front a closely packed planting of bush roses. The effect was a solid phalanx of blooms; like a seedsman's catalogue, it looked too good to be true! It may have been the absolute perfection of this bed which made me critical of some of the others.

'Deep Secret', very dark red and my favourite colour, was spectacular. It is less tall and more robust than 'Papa Meilland' and not so lowly and spreading as I find 'Josephine Bruce'. The blooms when fully out are quartered, the foliage suitably dark. It is not so scented as its two rivals, but enough to please me.

Two other beds were spectacularly pleasing. 'Helen Traubel' was introduced in 1951, so has been even longer in favour than 'Wendy Cussons'. The foliage was shiny, and the abundant blooms—which open quite widely when mature, almost the size of 'Peace' here—were a light apricot pink, a sort of shell-like salmon-pink, the older blooms having a trace of yellow at the base. The stems were strong, and the blooms were nicely upright and very scented. In another bed, and equally pleasing, was 'Lady Johnson', very like 'Helen Traubel', and similarly fragrant, but more delicate, with darker blooms—seemingly the same colour, but with more paint from the palette. If I were making a garden with subtle colour grading I might have four beds, with 'Peace' in the first, then 'Helen Traubel', then 'Lady Johnson' and finally 'Troika'.

There was a good bed of 'Troika' in Regents Park—though it is the sort of very strong vermilion-orange rose that I do not favour. Introduced in 1972, it is described in the Rose Society's *Selected List of Varieties* as 'light apricot to orange, edged and veined scarlet, full (29 petals), fragrant'. It has some single blooms and some in clusters. It is vigorous and upright, with glossy foliage. Sam McGredy, in his book *Look to the Rose* (Collins, 1982), says of 'Troika': 'One of the very best roses in the world to-day. It has about everything—colour, fragrance, constitution and health . . . the plant is of ideal habit, branching freely and flowering continuously. The colour is in the range of bronzy blends which have been the fashion of the late 70's. Above all it has a rich strong fragrance.'

There was also a magnificent bed of 'Mme Louis Laperrière'. This deep crimson rose was introduced in 1951. It is of moderate height and vigour, and the blooms when open are richly fragrant. With its dark foliage and a dark cloudy sky this rose had a deep, mysterious atmosphere. I loved it and added it to my catalogue of worthwhile dark reds. It has a reputation for being a good bedder.

All the Hybrid Tea roses in the Queen Mary's Garden were planted very closely together. Not only does this smother every possible weed but it leaves no possible room for any ground cover you might want with them. This is a very costly way of growing roses, especially as the amount of food they would need each year

This closely planted bed of 'Wendy Cussons' was glorious, a solid phalanx of blooms. The way it was arranged— with standards behind and bush roses in front—was also very effective.

Opposite: Growing in the circular centre bed in Queen Mary's Rose Garden was 'Troika', according to Sam McGredy 'one of the very best roses in the world today'.

obviously means that they must be freshly planted out at least every two years. It is also an artificial way of growing roses, but a very effective one for the visitor to parks.

Amongst the old shrub roses, there was a very pretty grouping of 'Fantin-Latour'. This has $3\frac{1}{2}$-inch (9cm), cup-shaped, pale pink flowers, opening flat with a button eye, and growing in clusters of four or five. The bushes were more than 6 feet (1.8m) high and 6 feet (1.8m) across. The roses were growing closely together, and were a delicate pastel pink—the painter having used quite a lot of Chinese white when he made his mixture. The petals were fluted and the roses adorable. They were out of a Fragonard picture, and I expected a lady in a crinoline on a swing to float between them towards me. (Fletcher restrain yourself, how could a lady in a crinoline get on to a swing?) The outer petals of this rose are large, and enfold the closely packed, much shorter, fluted centre ones. Its picture is on p. 18.

Here also was 'Constance Spry'—the new old rose, introduced in 1961, and flowering vigorously. The colour is a deep glowing pink in the centre of the large, fragrant, globular flowers, and pale pink outside, with long shoots up to 6 feet (2.4m). She is well supported here by her neighbours, but she does need imaginative help in this direction, as the sheer weight of the flowers bears her down.

Another rose which gave me great pleasure that afternoon was 'Climbing Malaga'. It was climbing one of those very attractive trellis pillars, here connected with each other by ropes garlanded with roses. It is on these pillars and ropes that the climbers and ramblers are seen to perfection; they also house quite a few of the taller old-fashioned shrub roses and, of course, the pillar roses. 'Climbing Malaga' had the whole trellis pillar to itself. The roses were large, fully out and floppy—had I been a day later, all would have been over. The double, fragrant blooms are a salmon-pink with carmine reverse. 'Copenhagen' was one of its parents: this is one of my favourite pillar roses, 10 feet (3m) at most. We have it against a

A feature of the Queen Mary's Rose Garden—pillars and swagged ropes.

pierced concrete wall in our TV Garden at Kings Heath Park, Birmingham, from whence my twelve-year-old TV weekly programme comes which I share with Bob Price, that most endearing of all garden experts, and by now a dear friend. 'Copenhagen' was his idea—it is a favourite of his too. It bears large floppy flowers of pale crimson, gloriously fragrant, and it seems to bloom the whole summer. Neither of these roses should be over-vigorous in growth; both would be excellent for the small garden.

'Chaplin's Pink Companion' was also seen to tremendous advantage on several of the trellis pillars. It is a vigorous climber of silvery salmon pink; introduced in 1961, it looks Victorian. Alas it is not recurrent, but it flowers for a long period.

In another of the wedge-shaped beds was 'Just Joey'. Now I was given three bushes of 'Just Joey' a few years ago at an awkward time for me, as my rose garden as such was full to bursting and I had to find a home for these three bushes. In the end they were reluctantly housed in a shrubbery bed in front of a blue cupressus hybrid and behind the hardy pink-leaved *Fuchsia magellanica* 'Versicolor'— this obliging shrub changes the shading of its leaves from pink to grey-green, and almost has a purple-pink-green effect like a dress material I believe is called 'shot taffeta'. Well the poor things were cramped there, although the wonderful light coppery orange of the flowers was gem-like between the blue and the green/pink/purple. 'Small insignificant little blooms', I thought, 'of a lovely colour!' Then I met 'Just Joey' at Regents Park: enormous translucent blooms of copper-orange. 'What's this?' I said to myself, and getting nearer there was the name. I found it difficult to associate them with my cheeky little blooms, which seemed so right for the name 'Just Joey'. These seemed as if they should be called 'Ah Josephine', with a little awe in the voice. Now if I added a fifth bed to the colour spectrum of roses I just imagined, I think 'Just Joey' should be placed between 'Lady Johnson' and 'Troika'. It's funny, but until this visit to the Queen Mary's Garden at Regents Park I had not greatly cared for these orange, rusty pink roses, and here I am head over heels about them.

I would like to describe the design of the Queen Mary's Garden for those who have not been there. One enters by some very beautiful ornamental wrought-iron gates (the Jubilee Gates) and turns left, and then one is entering what is in effect a circular garden. The focal point of the garden is a circular centre bed, about 25 feet ($7\frac{1}{2}$m) across (here 'Troika' was growing). Then there is a wide path, perhaps 10 feet (3m), and then grass in which have been cut long wedge-shaped beds which complete, in segments, another larger circle. Then there is more grass and finally the white-panelled trellis towers, about 15 feet ($4\frac{1}{2}$m) high, between which are thick looped ropes garlanded by climbing roses, thus making a tall circle of roses to contain all. Behind these at random are other beds, some of Hybrid Teas, some of the shrub and species roses, and a path leading up to and away from the main circle has many thickly planted rose beds on either side. It is not an enormous garden, but it is elegant and satisfying in its classical simplicity.

THE GARDENS AT LIME KILN

Lime Kiln Garden, at Claydon in Suffolk, was first planted with roses by Countess Sophie Benckendorff in the 1920s. It is now largely a garden planted and created by Humphrey Brooke. In 1956 that distinguished American gardener, Mr Lanning Roper, planner of many of our most beautiful gardens, was staying there, and he suggested how it could be revived and planted. Humphrey Brooke had begun his plantings in the summer of 1954, when he bought Lime Kiln. He planted sixty-two Hybrid Teas in his first summer holiday. Largely because of the soil they did not flourish, and it was then that Lanning Roper suggested the old roses.

The main emphasis is on remontant, or recurrent groups, especially Hybrid (or Victorian) Perpetuals, together with Chinas, Hybrid Chinas, Bourbons, Noisettes, Teas, early Hybrid Teas, Rugosas, Hybrid Musks and Polyanthas.

All the colours blend happily together, and there has been no attempt to group the roses according to colour. There is one bed that is an exception, where mauve, lavender, soft pink, primrose, apricot and buff are the colours chosen. These colours, Humphrey Brooke told me, were the ones worn by his young daughter, who sadly died of heat-stroke in Portugal in her seventeenth summer. 'It occupied my mind at this time to make a new garden and have it as her memorial,' he went on. Here there are 166 varieties of roses undersown with forget-me-nots for the spring and regale lilies for later in the summer.

Humphrey Brooke told me that he was a manic depressive. He was told by a leading psychiatrist that all geniuses from Shakespeare to Churchill were manic depressives, who created masterpieces in their non-depressive phases. He said that he was not a genius, but he feels that had he not suffered from this disease his garden would not be what it is today! Humphrey Brooke, in his late sixties, looks like a genius and approaches one with the assured air of a man who knows. He is a renowned expert, and surrounded by 500 bushes of outstanding beauty, all of his own collection and creation, he proves himself and his gardens to be living legends. He is also highly unconventional in his attitude to the culture of his precious possessions. He does not prune, he does not spray, he does not use artificial fertilizers and he rarely uses manure. All he does is to deadhead as much as possible (several hours a day after peak flowering). He does a careful cutting back when dead-heading, and he attaches some bushes and branches to each other with soft string; he also makes use of the trees and the old brick walls as support. This he calls 'presentation'.

The whole garden was a riot of roses and bloom when we arrived. It was gloriously untidy with the roses in 'rolling waves, scented and magnificent', wrote Anita Pereire in the popular French magazine *Madame Figaro* in February 1981. '*L'Etonnant Secret d'un Collectionneur de Roses—il ne taille* [prune] *jamais: Lime Kiln n'est pas une roseraie, c'est un jungle de roses.*' 'A jungle of roses', he says, 'that has been my intent.' A Californian publication, *Heritage Rose*, wrote in 1978 that Lime Kiln was 'the highlight of a tour of all the principal rose gardens and nurseries in Europe'.

Opposite: In June 1981 this *R. californica plena* in Lime Kiln Garden carried 8,000 blooms. Now count how many in 1982.

Certainly it is the quaintest. One is completely overwhelmed by the size of the bushes. As you wander in this overgrown and scented space, you have to weave your way through the trailing bushes. I swear some clutched me as I passed, demanding that I looked long and deeply into their enchanting faces.

Not being pruned, the roses have accordingly grown to their natural size. The supposedly dwarf 'Perle d'Or' (1883) is 8 feet 6 inches (2.5m) high and carried about 700 blooms. 'Souvenir de la Malmaison' (1843), growing by the drive, is nearly 20 feet (6m) in diameter and is normally in bloom till Christmas. *R. californica plena* carried approximately 8,000 blooms in June and July 1981. Over the years these roses have grown into positive fortress walls of green and colour, while a wild tangle of flowering roses falls from the trees. One can imagine this old wizard, Humphrey Brooke, padding his way with sandalled feet at five in the morning (he works in the garden for two hours till seven) and savouring the dew on the soft roses at dawn.

Because there are no Hybrid Tea roses here, and because the

Humphrey Brooke and myself standing beneath 'Cerise Bouquet', which has a growth up to 9 feet (2.7m), we are told. I am exactly 6 feet (1.8m), so this rose must be about 18 foot high at Lime Kiln, with a strong, exquisite scent

Hybrid Tea is the accepted shape of rose to the man in the street, this joyous gardener finds great amusement in the reactions of some visitors, who arrive in coachloads. A whole lot of wild species roses from different parts of the world flank the right-hand side of the lawn as one enters. Here is a tumbling cascade of rich pink blossoms from the 18-foot (5.6m) tall *R. californica plena*. In one case the leader of a coachload was heard to say, 'That isn't a rose! We've come to the wrong place! About turn!' and they left. Mr Brooke has now christened this the Turnabout Rose, because so many coach passengers turn away when they see it. As opposed to the coachloads, Mr Brooke thinks the Hybrid Teas 'are the colour of squashed oranges and covered with black spot'. It takes all kinds for the rose nurseryman to please!

We talked in an arbour with a Norfolk reed roof—although the reeds were hardly visible because of the generosity of 'May Queen' almost completely covering it with her pale-pink blooms. Cascading over the trees in the orchard was 'Paul's Himalayan Musk', 30 feet (9m) high at least and blush pink in colour, and a similar mountain of blossom was provided by *R. moschata plena*, an old sixteenth-century rose with trusses of fragrant, off-white flowers. 'Goldfinch', a less vigorous rambler but very free-flowering, was a mixture of golden yellow and primrose with richly coloured anthers and a gloriously heavy scent. Opposite the waterfall of bloom provided by 'Paul's Himalayan Musk' was an even higher mountain of scented blooms from the dark, warm pink 'Cerise Bouquet'. Pinkish crimson might describe these highly scented flowers. I have a catalogue by me which says modestly that this rose needs support! It is a modern shrub, first introduced in 1958 by Wilhelm Kordes: it is a good example of how the modern rose breeder has added, and will doubtless add in the future, 'new' 'old' roses to match in glory, and fit in well with, the old roses.

The whole garden was such a jungle that it was difficult to find one's way about to the best advantage. In the centre of an area where an asparagus bed had been excavated was a 16 feet (4.8m) high 'Lavender Lassie'. 'Why it should be called that', said Humphrey Brooke, 'when it is pink, I'll never know.' This, too, is a modern oldie, introduced by R. Kordes in 1959. It's a Hybrid Musk of Floribunda type; the flowers are double, borne in clusters and strongly scented. 'Rose de Rescht' is a good example of a quartered Pompon, while a small bush of 'Capitaine John Ingram' had double, rather globular flowers of dark crimson-purple, maturing to deepest maroon. This is a Moss rose, and the bud had a large mossy calyx; it is fragrant, and as you will see from the picture on p. 89 looks like a tiny dark paeony.

Another deep red was the Rugosa 'Mrs Anthony Waterer'. The shrub was 7 feet (2.1m) high, showing well against the old wall; it was scented, and there was some quite strong magenta in the crimson. Startlingly lovely, I thought. 'Great Western' had large maroon flowers; it is a vigorous Bourbon, with double, cupped flowers and a strong delicious scent. Their pictures are also on p. 89.

'Perle d'Or' is one of Lime Kiln's major glories, with its loosely floppy blossoms of pale apricot, gloriously scented. This was about 9

Above: 'Perle d'Or'. Supposedly dwarf, here at Lime Kiln it is over 8 feet (2.4m) high. Right: Growing against an old brick wall was 'Leverkusen', a vigorous modern shrub with sprays of pale yellow double flowers.

feet (2.7m) tall, with a myriad of blooms borne in clusters on the delicate brown stems. This is a Polyantha rose introduced in 1890. 'Amelia', in the memorial border, was an open, camellia-type rose of lavender-pink—such a subtle shade—an Alba with a strong scent but not recurrent. If I made a border of old shrub roses, I do not think I could be without her! 'Félicité Parmentier' was the palest shell pink, with a closely packed cup of petals. This was another Alba (1834), strongly scented, with grey-green foliage (see p. 89).

Though, alas, with no scent, 'Conditorum' was a fabulous, open, crimson-pink, semi-double Gallica. And here is a most useful yellow, 'Alchymist'. It is a small climbing rose with strongly scented, fully double blooms, a mixture of yellow and apricot. Unfortunately it is not recurrent. 'Belle Amour' is an Alba/Damask cross, with a most compelling perfume, almost of myrrh, perhaps because it was discovered in a convent garden! It is a tightly petalled, cupped rose of pale coral-pink. It cannot, alas, repeat this beautiful performance in the autumn.

Rosa 'Fisher Holmes' has a crimson richness, both in colour and scent, and he is also a recurrent Hybrid Perpetual. He would make a good solidly coloured background to a *R. dupontii*, which is a short lax climber with white to very pale pink flowers with outstandingly beautiful yellow stamens. This is one of our earliest roses, having a confused ancestry back to 1596. Michael Gibson says it is a Gallica hybrid with the Musk rose. It has a luxuriant musk perfume.

'Phyllis Bide' is an untidy, small rambler, but it nevertheless drew one's attention. Its charm was really in its small, slightly scented, semi-double flowers of beigy-white-apricot! It is a climbing Polyanthus, and in autumn its burgeon of flowers is darker in colour. It makes a very good weeping standard. 'Felicia' is a pastel shade of silvery salmon pink, a Hybrid Musk, recurrent and scented (see p. 10). 'Chianti' is a modern shrub rose of distinction. It is free-flowering with clusters of semi-double blooms of a rich purple-maroon, and a vigorous plant. It has enough scent to please me, but alas it is not recurrent. As its parents were 'Cardinal de Richelieu' and 'Dusty Maiden', it was obviously destined to have this rich luxuriant colour.*

There was a graceful rose against an old brick wall, a perpetual climber called 'Leverkusen', with double, pale yellow flowers, beautifully scented. It is a Kordesii hybrid introduced in 1954.

Gertrude Jekyll talks of a beneficence of overgrowth—Humphrey Brooke certainly has it. She also talks of 'an attractive charm about these older flowers that anyone who truly loves a garden must needs feel, though it may be hard to define'. Certainly, there is an attractive charm about Lime Kiln. This has been conjured from a hostile chalk soil by a devoted and artistic wizard in Humphrey Brooke. It was a golden afternoon to remember.

'Fisher Holmes' (Hybrid Perpetual).

---

* *Mr Graham Stuart Thomas—and who can doubt such an authority—says that the parents are* R. macrantha *and* 'Vanity'. *My information came from the* Dictionary of Roses *by Miller Gault and Patrick Synge (Michael Joseph, in collaboration with the Royal Horticultural Society and the Royal National Rose Society; 3rd ed. 1980).*

BEES ROSE FIELDS

I am now going to write about the rose fields of a large commercial grower and breeder with many, many acres of roses. In one field were 1½ million roses and in another nearby were 840,000. These were at Sealand near Chester, the rose fields and nurseries of that well-known and long-established horticultural firm Bees of Chester.

It was a sunny day in July, and Michael Warren and I were there to take pictures of the 'Cyril Fletcher' rose. It was a proud and magic moment for me to see rows and rows of my rose glistening happily and fragrantly in the flat field, very open to the sky—and what an odd coincidence that next to the rows of the 'Cyril Fletcher' rose were several rows of that lovable little Floribunda 'Ballerina'. My wife Betty Astell started her professional career as a student with the Diaghilev Ballet, so here we were side by side.

Visiting a rose nursery is a wonderful experience. Here might be ten rows each a hundred yards long of 'Super Star' or 'Whisky Mac', then another whole block of 'Silver Jubilee' or 'Alpine Sunset'. At one side, against a hedge, and growing to 4 feet (1.2m) or more, were the very healthy, profuse, long-lasting blooms of 'Alexander'. These roses are described in the catalogues as brilliant vermilion. I have always thought of them as the same bright red as a cornfield poppy, and there in the hedgerow to prove my point was a large group of wild cornfield poppies, exactly the same colour.

When you see hundreds, nay thousands, of Hybrid Teas and Floribundas in flower, at your feet and then stretching out away from you, even as far as the horizon, it is an amazing sight. Many leading nurseries have open days, and are well worth a visit.

After savouring all this beauty we went to the power-house—in other words to the greenhouse, by private garden standards enormous—where Tony Hallows, the expert breeder for Bees, holds sway and makes magic. Here were regiments of bushes, all with labels as to who had married whom, and in the centre, as the picture on p.74 shows, an enormously long bed of this year's seedlings—some marked with canes as promising, some yet to flower, some full of hope and some of despair. Tony Hallows will sow in a year 2,000 seeds, from which, if he is lucky, may come a selection of 150 roses as his first choice. These will be grown on and transplanted outside in the nursery for the next summer's flowering, and judging from the flowers, and from their behaviour in the open after a hard winter, he may perhaps be blessed with five possibles; a good year might provide a dozen. Tony Hallows is a large cheerful man with a philosophical smile—and I think he needs it. His job has more disappointments than most—though this must make his successes all the more enjoyable and memorable. After all he was midwife to Rose Number 7003. That is the 'Cyril Fletcher' rose. My parents, surprisingly, were 'Fragrant Cloud' and 'Whisky Mac', and I was born in 1973. My Trial Ground number at Bone Hill—as this book is published I am in my second exciting year—is 5370. Go and look at me. Smell me: my aroma is exotic. Then of course buy me and plant me in your garden. Talk to me from time to time. If you hear the faintest murmur in the air in rhyme, it will be me answering back!

Opposite: Cyril is given a bloom of the 'Cyril Fletcher' rose by Cliff Staples of Bees amongst acres of their roses. Standing in these fields of roses, the scent is perhaps the first thing that astonishes, and then the various bands of colour produced by the different varieties of rose, each in its own section. The effect of the bands of colour is worth noticing. In your mind's eye a certain rose has its own definite colour, in your own particular private spectrum of colour as it were. When you see literally thousands of blooms of that colour all merging together and disappearing into the distance, that colour is intensified.

10

The Royal National Rose Society

The advantages for a keen amateur rosarian in having an active society to enlarge and encourage his enthusiasm for his hobby are obvious. The Royal National Rose Society, founded in 1876, is a strong society with a fascinating history which, through the years, traces the evolution of our present-day roses, with as far back as 1884 pleas from eminent rose growers and exhibitors (in the *Rosarians' Year Book*) to encourage 'the old-fashioned roses'.

The first President and Secretary—indeed the founders of the Society—were two clergymen: Dean—at that time Canon—Reynolds Hole (who amongst other things was a keen follower of hounds), and the Revd Honeywood D'ombrain. These two, together with Mr Edward Mawley (who became joint Hon. Secretary), dominated the Society for the next thirty years. Dean Hole died in 1904 aged eighty-five, and D'ombrain two years later aged eighty-seven. By then the Society had realized many of its objectives. There were 900 members, and the Society had established itself as the foremost authority on roses. It had through its frequent shows and awards, and its encouragement to breeders, greatly advanced the quality of the Hybrid Tea and decorative roses.

The year 1901 saw the move of the Annual Show from the Crystal Palace to the Gardens of the Inner Temple; in 1902 came the publication of the Society's *Select List of Varieties*, and in 1907 the first edition of the *Rose Annual*. In 1904 the Summer Show moved to Regents Park and the first Autumn Show to the Royal Horticultural Society Hall in Vincent Square. The rose had begun to assume its place as Queen of the Garden. By 1915 membership was 6,000.

In 1916 Mr Courtney Page began a long reign as joint Hon.

Right: Headquarters of the Royal National Rose Society, Bone Hill. The Princess Mary Rose Walk leads from the house to the pond.

Secretary. Under his editorship the size and range of the *Annual* increased. In 1927 part of his garden at Haywards Heath became the first Trial Ground of the Society. Breeders were invited to submit new roses not yet in commerce, and the successful ones received the 'Trial Ground Certificate'. The Society survived the war in the capable hands of Mr Courtney Page, who died in 1947. Mr Edland then became the first paid, full-time Secretary, and a new Trial Ground was opened at Oaklands near St Albans.

In 1960 the tenancy of the Society's premises in Victoria ran out and the Society moved to Bone Hill, St Albans. Here for the first time was a Display Garden, in which all the varieties awarded a Trial Ground Certificate were planted, together with a wide selection of old and modern shrub roses. Here also was the new Trial Ground

The purpose of the Trial Ground procedure is to judge new varieties not for their exhibition potential or their commercial possibilities, but solely as to their value as garden plants. This alone is a perfect reason for the existence of the RNRS. The roses are judged over a period of three years, and they come both from professional breeders and from amateurs. (The award for the most fragrant rose of 1981 went to 'Sheila's Perfume', which was bred by John Sheridan, an amateur breeder from London.) Six of each shrub, bush and miniature rose and two of each climber are judged, being identified only by their Trial Ground number. In 1981 approximately 500 different varieties were on trial.

The roses are judged by a panel of sixteen, plus the President. Points are awarded as follows:

Health, up to 20 points
Vigour and habit, up to 20 points
Form of bloom or cluster and colour, up to 20 points
General effect, continuity of flower, novelty, up to 30 points
Fragrance, up to 10 points

Apparently the most variable factor in the judges' markings is fragrance. Not only do their nose-holes have different wavelengths, as we have already discussed, but scent is affected by weather conditions, so that a rose might smell quite differently on a humid day and a dry windy day. What a terribly difficult job this is! (To me, by the way, 'Fragrant Cloud' is not a great smeller—obviously from the name I am wrong. Now Harkness in his catalogue gives 'Fragrant Cloud' 9 out of 10 for fragrance. To me 'Prima Ballerina' and 'Ernest H. Morse' have a very strong fragrance. Harkness gives 'E. H. Morse' 5 and 'Prima Ballerina' 8. I personally rate both of them higher than 'Fragrant Cloud'.)

The judges make four or more visits each, involving many hours of painstaking work. They work in groups of four and compare notes at the end of each examination. At the end of the three years the rose with the highest number of marks is awarded the President's International Trophy. The next award is the Certificate of Merit, and then the Trial Ground Certificate. The most scented rose is then awarded the Henry Edland Memorial Medal. The Torridge award is for the best rose bred by an amateur.

Opposite: A view of the Trial Ground at Bone Hill. Here new varieties of roses are judged over a period of three years.

'Maigold' flowers twice a year
prodigiously and is
beautifully scented—an ideal
rose for growing on a pillar.

In this important way the Royal National Rose Society is a great help to the keen amateur. When he is ordering new roses not only does he choose them because their colour fits in with his scheme, and their height and form are right for the particular place he wants them for in his garden; he also takes into account how the roses performed in the Trial Ground, and if he chooses roses that have received awards he will know that his choices will do well. With the aid of the reports in the *Rose Annual*, he will also be able to find out which roses will do best in a wet season and in a dry season and under all sorts of trials and tribulations.

The *Rose Annual* is a tremendous boon to the amateur. It is a handsome volume with excellent colour photographs; articles by learned experts and sometimes painstaking and sometimes frivolous amateurs; reports of the shows and other activities of the Society. If a keen rose grower is beset with troubles, be they business or family or just the state of his rose garden, I guarantee that the day the *Rose Annual* arrives his load will be lightened at least for a day or so as he browses contentedly through its informative pages.

Members can also obtain advice on any subject connected with roses by writing to the Secretary. There is an extensive reference library at Bone Hill. As the number of roses sold each year is about 35 million, the Rose Society faces a monster task, but it nevertheless succeeds in maintaining and continually improving the service it provides for members. Join!

The first Royal Patron of the Society was Queen Alexandra (her love of roses is perpetuated in Alexandra's Rose Day). Queen Mary followed her, and her daughter the Princess Royal followed her mother. The present Patron is Her Majesty Queen Elizabeth the Queen Mother, who is a most knowledgeable rosarian and keen gardener. In 1980 I designed a garden for Capital Radio at the Chelsea Flower Show and the Queen Mother, gallantly peering through a plastic cloche-type umbrella, came round in the pouring rain. In my garden I had a collection of shrub roses provided for me by Mattocks of Oxford and, undaunted by the weather, Her Majesty discussed their merits and habits and floriferousness in very expert detail. It was a memorable moment for me.

'Mme Hardy' is a Damask rose, heavily scented with a trace of lemon and with a lemon green eye in the centre of a generous double white bloom. This is considered by some to be the most beautiful of all white roses. First introduced 150 years ago.

BONE HILL—THE GARDEN OF THE ROYAL NATIONAL ROSE SOCIETY

When Watford—now, alas, almost a suburb of London—was a small market town I was born there. Now, four miles (6½km) away from Watford, into the deep quiet of Hertfordshire (yes, it can be surprisingly deep countryside as it benefits from the Green Belt), up a narrow country lane—Chiswell Green Lane—is 'Bone Hill', the garden of the Royal National Rose Society.

You would expect that the gardens of one of the oldest rose societies in the world would be perfect, that the roses in them would be perfect, and of every conceivable variety and species. They are. All is most beautifully done. They are near to London, they are easy to get at; at the same time they are in the heart of the country. If you are someone who is allergic to the catering of corporate bodies there is a little village and a pub nearby. For those of you who do not mind 'catering', then it is capable, adequate and friendly. One does not ask these days how many gardeners someone employs, if any, so one hesitates to estimate how many highly qualified and vigorous gardeners are employed at Bone Hill—but certainly enough to keep the roses growing in pristine glory.

I am someone who has admired and adored and been positively potty about roses all his life and yet I had not been to this Mecca of rosarians before I visited it for this book in June 1982. I had been meaning to go, having been a member of the RNRS for twenty odd years or so. My sister lives quite near, so it would have been a very easy progression. I think I shied away feeling that I might be disappointed. I might choose a day following a week of battering rain and wind and be completely put off the hallowed ground for life. I did! and I was not!

The summer had started early and hot, with weeks of continuous sunshine in May, but these were followed by Ascot and Wimbledon and rain. The wettest June, we heard, since records had been kept—well, since last June anyway. I had chosen a day of high cloud, not much wind and a nice feeling of sunshine after rain. The sun did not come out a lot; for roses I feel it needs to. I certainly did not give

**Miniature roses are grown
in a small side garden at
Bone Hill, on terrace shelves.**

myself enough time. You need to be eagerly at the gate at opening time and you need to stay and gloat and admire and sniff and pry and write down daft, inadequate descriptions for which you need a definite separate note book (the back of the gas bill envelope soon gets inadequate!). You also need a camera and rolls of coloured film. I was lucky. I had the willing, artistic, equally fascinated and very knowledgeable camera belonging to Michael Warren, an enthusiastic artist and gardener if ever there was one. He made the visit even more enjoyable. At one time I suffered from a TV producer (nothing to do with my present programme, whose producer John Pullen is enthusiastic and the epitome of co-operation) who hated any suggestions I made for a picture and took only those I wanted taken as 'how not to do it'. I only twigged this on the second day unfortunately, and then by asking for what I didn't want I got what I did! You can imagine how an artistic enterprise suffered from this. I like to think that the pictures in this book are especially good because Michael got to know what I wanted and brought his special flair and knowledge and expertise to bring it off.

We arrived. Immediately on entering I was overwhelmed by the beauty of this, the beauty of that. I dashed here and there, looked

A typical view at Bone Hill: 'Charlotte Elizabeth', 'Vera Dalton', and 'Chaplin's Pink Companion' on the pergola.

closely at this, and breathed in the individual perfume of that. Looked at something else from afar and gloried in the all-over picture. It was almost like a blind man being given sudden sight. What do we look at first, where do we start? Take a picture of this. No that—and all the time I knew at the back of my mind that my book would contain a maximum of sixty pictures, and this was our third garden. We took 360 pictures of Bone Hill alone. (Yes Mr Collins, there is another whole book there!!)

Now a little calmer Mr Fletcher please. A little more orderly. It was like meeting the most appreciative audience in the world and you could not decide which joke or which Odd Ode to tell them first.

The Pillar Roses

We began at the entrance to the long, curved walk, first opening on the left. One is welcomed here by a semi-circle of gravel path round which is more of a semi-circular pergola than an arch. This makes for a grander entrance—something that could well be repeated at the entrance to any rose garden. Up and over it, flowering at its very best, was 'Chaplin's Pink Companion'. Each pillar supported a different rose—all presumably designed to give a long show. 'Parkdirektor Riggers', with its single red blooms of great staying power for later on in the season; 'Maigold', whose bronze blooms give scented pleasure now and later, and in the bed 'Robusta', a vigorous red rose, with single flowers. Introduced by Kordes in 1982, it is a repeat flowering shrub rose.

Through beds of Floribunda roses on either side of the path we came to another circle—complete this time—of pillars, a kind of temple of roses serving as the entrance to the long pergola of roses. Here there are forty-six different kinds of climbing and rambler roses. It would be wrong to describe each one inadequately—some in any case were not completely at their best: the early ones were, the late ones were yet to come. 'Golden Showers' was not over tall, but flowering generously with yellow fading to almost white flowers which will continue all summer (see p. 89). 'Seagull' was magnificent in several different places (see p. 37); we later saw it growing and flowering strongly by the pond. This is a very vigorous rambler; the flowers are single white with yellow stamens and sufficiently large to appear almost double from a distance. It is not recurrent unfortunately, but in a garden where 'Kiftsgates'' extreme vigour would be overwhelming 'Seagull' could be contained, and the flowers are very much bigger. Then there was *R. longicuspis*, very similar to my favourite *R. filipes* 'Kiftsgate'; it is equally vigorous and equally scented.

A very effective pillar rose was 'Parade', with carmine Hybrid Tea-like blooms, recurrent and growing to 12 feet (3.6m). It was heavily laden with very scented flowers, large and double, which drooped slightly. Although it looks deliciously old-fashioned it was introduced from America in 1953. Another pillar housed 'Dortmund'. This has large crimson-red flowers with a white eye and heavy yellow stamens. It is recurrent so long as you dead-head the clustered flowers, otherwise large heps will inhibit the second flowering. I thought this flower had a very attractive peppery—

almost lupin-like—fragrance and I loved it.

Two yellow roses adorning the pillars were 'Lawrence Johnston' and 'Mermaid'. 'Lawrence Johnston' was the creator of that magical Cotswold garden, Hidcote. To see it there, his rose is not a rose to be remarked upon, rather feeble and straggly against one of his Cotswold walls—but to see it at Bone Hill vigorously bright yellow, swarming as in the picture on p. 31 with loose yellow blooms, strongly scented and flinging its yellow ribbons in the air against the sky, was to see a rose as magic as the garden it comes from—with Hidcote Lavender and Hidcote Hypericum (it was this lovely colour). It will grow to 20 feet (6m). 'Mermaid' is sulphur-yellow and best in full sun as it was here. A dainty but large single rose which flowers all summer. This glorious, delicately scented rose will grow to 30 feet (9m) in height.

Growing very strongly on one pillar—though not tall enough to go across the bar—was 'Hamburger Phoenix'; it is very redly crimson—a bright crimson—the flowers semi-double with a slight scent. If you needed a dramatic exclamation mark in your garden the closely growing flowers of this strong red rose would provide it. And it does not fade. You would have to be very careful where you planted this rose so as not to let it overwhelm the colours of its neighbours. It would be perfect against a small grey stone house.

Some Wonderful Displays

Away from the pergola, climbing a standard tripod made of rustic wood, was 'Chaplin's Pink Companion' again, in front of which a genius had planted 'Erfurt'. This is a Hybrid Musk, recurrent, with a very long flowering period. It has pink and white flowers, and a good scent. To one side was 'Hunter'—not so inspired a choice; it is scarlet-crimson as the name suggests, a vigorous hybrid Rugosa shrub, recurrent but scentless. It is a John Mattock rose which would have been better used as a hedge.

Another outstanding combination of two roses—the sort of picture one carries in one's mind for a long time—was 'Elizabeth Arden' and 'Saga'. 'Saga' has lovely buff-tinted white flowers, semi-double and fragrant, in generous clusters. 'Elizabeth Arden' is a pink and white Floribunda, fragrant with very attractive pointed buds.

A bed of 'Red Fountain' was magnificent and had withstood the rain remarkably well. Then there was a bed of 'Korresia', a very unfading yellow rose with reasonable fragrance. It made a good picture against its dark bronzy foliage. 'Iceberg' in a bed on its own showed what a wonderfully individual and superior rose this is. So very floriferous, such large, light, airy roses and so many in each cluster; some were open showing the yellow stamens, some completely closed, and some buds tipped with the faintest pink, all on open, spreading bushes. This bed was of exceptional beauty and impossible to describe!

The 'City of Leeds' roses massed in their long bed were magnificent. It has semi-double, salmon-pink, Hybrid Tea-type blooms, which open out later. It is a very rich salmon enhanced tremendously by its bronze young foliage. Very little scent I'm afraid. And there was the bed of magenta/beetroot-red roses, 'News', that I have already described in Chapter 8.

Oh, and I must mention 'Aloha'. This is a modern shrub introduced in 1949. It is a voluptuous rose of sixty or so rose-pink petals with a deeper reverse. It can be grown as a pillar rose or a large shrub. It is free-flowering, recurrent and highly scented. It was perfection when we visited it—and though its Hybrid Tea flowers fade to blush pink on the outside as it ages, its centre becomes a sort of dark, weathered brick pink. It is unusual and lovely, and there was a lot of it.

The 'Roses of Romance'

The roses we met in the section of the garden devoted to what C. E. Lucas Phillips calls the Roses of Romance (why are soldiers so artistically romantic?) were at the height of their beautiful perfection. Bone Hill has a most excellent and comprehensive collection. The Society owes much to the scholarship and devotion of Mr Graham Thomas here; not only is he the greatest living authority on the old roses, but he has earned the Society's gratitude for his help with this almost definitive collection.

There are only a few quiet pastel yellows here—otherwise all is white and pink and maroon, velvety textures, open roses, camellia rosette-like roses and heavy-headed cabbages; all scented, all evocative of their history, all giving us an atmosphere of their gracious past, with the sun giving by now a patina of summer happiness.

I would like to give you pictures of them all. Michael Warren takes portraits of roses; he shows their character and their allure. Look at his picture of 'President de Sèze' (p. 61)—can you not smell the fragrance as you look deeply into its pinkish-purple quartered blooms, that are frequently 4 inches (10cm) across? This is a French rose introduced in 1836; it has given us 146 years of delight.

These are the roses of the poets. When they sang of the red rose it was not the strident colours of 'Fragrant Cloud' or 'Lovers Meeting' or 'Troika' (praise this rose as I have earlier on) they had in mind. The poets sang of rich purples, lilacs and what I personally call black maroons. (It sounds almost like an old Scottish regiment!) These deep, dusky, mysterious colours suffer a sun-change into something rich and strange, they fade to the smoky mauves of distant hills. Let us look at one of them. On p. 6 is 'Tuscany Superb', a Gallica sometimes known as the Old Velvet Rose; it is not as highly scented as the double blooms of deepest crimson-purple suggest, nor as scented as 'Rose du Roi'. This is a Damask or a Hybrid Perpetual—no one can decide which. He was raised as a seedling in 1812 in the gardens of St Cloud, and his fragrance is as rich as his crimson-purple colour. Mr Harkness claims never to have seen one—though his nursery is at Hitchin, a few miles from St Albans, and he visits the Trial Ground so often; also Mr Humphrey Brooke has it at Lime Kiln. Or have I stumbled upon one of those gardening arguments which have been the mainstay of BBC's *Gardener's Question Time* for years? As we used to watch *What's my Line?* to see if Gilbert Harding was in recalcitrant mood, so we listen to *Gardener's*

Question Time to see if they are arguing!

Another Damask, an outstanding rose in every way, was 'Mme Hardy'. Look at the innocence of her portrait (p. 113), pure white, very double and very fragrant, so elegant in growth. She has been delighting her audience since 1832, and is regarded by some as 'the most beautiful white rose in existence'. I thought she smelt strongly as a rose close to, and distantly as a lemon. I am going to digress here and say that I certainly think she is *one* of the two most beautiful white roses in existence. The other grew on my grey-stone Sussex wall: it was a pillar rose, alas not too floriferous but recurrent, 'White Cockade', introduced by J. Cocker, a lovely Hybrid Tea shape and nicely scented. I do sometimes think, however, that owning a thing enhances it in the owner's eyes!

Now let's choose a pink, 'Félicité Parmentier', with a touch of salmon in the palest pink of all. An Alba rose, introduced in 1834, highly scented, a compact shrub with grey-green foliage (see p. 89). A slightly brighter pink, with such a warm profusion of petals surrounding a green button, was 'Königin von Danemarck'. This too is an Alba, with quartered blooms and a rich, strong scent.

R. alba semi-plena I show you as a picture of a lovely single rose (see p. 13). Who could resist these waved petals in perfect form and shape round the bright yellow anthers? This Alba rose dates from the sixteenth century, and the flowers are richly scented.

'Ferdinand Pichard' is a Hybrid Perpetual, and to my mind the most attractive of the striped varieties. The flowers are a double pale pink striped with crimson, in spite of its look of antiquity it was introduced in 1921 (see p. 68). It is scented and free flowering. 'Fantin-Latour' is a splendid, if not *the*, example of a Centifolia rose (see p. 18). It has blush pink, highly fragrant flowers, and is abundantly floriferous. The blooms are cup-shaped and many-petalled, and grow in clusters; the petals towards the centre of the rose are a deeper shell-pink in colour. It was much liked by the painter after

'Red Fountain', a repeat flowering shrub rose, had withstood the rain remarkably well.

'Hamburger Phoenix' was growing strongly on one pillar at Bone Hill. If you needed a dramatic exclamation mark in your garden this bright crimson, unfading rose would provide it.

whom it was named. And, of course, there was my favourite Moss rose, 'William Lobb', Old Velvet Moss, with his thickly mossed buds and large purple-magenta blooms heavy with scent (see p. 65).

As we entered there was a Rugosa hedge, with some lovely Rugosas: 'Roseraie de l'Hay' (p. 41), steadily flowering through the summer with purple flowers and strong purple fragrance. How can you have a purple fragrance I wonder? I know what I mean as I write it but later on like God and Mr Browning I may be wondering what I mean! Look at the picture of *R. rugosa alba* (p. 38). How perfect a rose is she, hardy, vigorous and scented, with red heps and yellow foliage in the autumn too. The Rugosas do not have the elegance of the other old roses—they are too rustic-looking and hardy—but they are very trouble-free.

The shrub roses at Bone Hill suffer in a way from too much space. Large beds allow large, lax, lazy shrubs to fall into each other, each enormous bed sporting a separate kind.

Along the southern and eastern boundaries of the display garden are the wild roses and their offspring. They vary in habit from the immense climbers to ground coverers. The flowers are many but small and single. The foliage is often different and spectacular, like the fern-like foliage of *R. primula*, with a rich incense which makes you retrace your steps to find out the whereabouts of the censer. And again there is *R. rubrifolia*, now grey, now blue, now plum colour— all on the same spray sometimes. Here I suppose is a corner all on its own for the botanist and the breeder, and also for the enquiring person who wants to know more about the history of the rose and its roots and whence it came. 'Canary Bird' was over, but there was a hybrid from *R. spinosissima*—'Frühlingsschnee', with large, single, creamy white flowers on a thorny bush, disease-free, and very scented.

The Pool and the Miniatures

From the house there is a long paved walk known as the Princess Mary Rose Walk, lined with beds of Floribundas. This takes us to the pool, with the pergolas on either side of it. Princess Mary was President of the Society when she opened Bone Hill. The pool is fringed with the modern shrub rose 'Ballerina' (see p. 43). A rose with large sprays of small pink single blossoms with a white centre, and a long period of bloom, she is short and spreads in a way no ballerina would be allowed to. With 'Ballerina' is 'Yesterday', another modern shrub, low and bushy with sprays of tiny lavender-pink semi-double flowers. It is nearly always in scented bloom. 'The Fairy' completes this trio, with small double flowers of soft pink; this is yet another modern shrub, repeat flowering, and $2\frac{1}{2}$ feet (75cm) high. With 'Seagull' towering high against the sky and all this beauty reflected in the pool, with water lilies and a fountain, it makes an enchanting centrepiece.

The miniature roses are grown in a small side garden. Almost as if on shelves, with retaining walls between each 'shelf', the dainty roses are well displayed, and made a pretty picture as we turned the corner.

At Bone Hill there is every kind of rose, all growing well and in good health. The lightish, gravelly soil is not the ideal soil for roses, so if they grow well here then they will grow well elsewhere. Their health and excellent quality of growth are a great tribute to the gardeners of the RNRS. Congratulations. Bone Hill is a venue for all rose lovers, and well worth many a visit at various times to relish every facet of the myriad inhabitants.

*   *   *

I have praised this glorious display of perfect roses. Also the fact that it is a definitive, representative collection of roses. Just everything is there, and well displayed. I found the pool and the pergola around it excellent. The Princess Mary Rose Walk with its sentinel Irish yews and beds of Floribundas is spectacular. The longer pergola walk is well furnished, and the proportions exactly right . . . but what a pity that the whole garden is so flat—no change of level anywhere, and a total absence of vast trees: no glorious specimen cedars, no ancient tulip trees, just a few large trees on the outskirts. Instead the sheer flatness and lack of trees gave us too open a look and too much sky.

The pool and pergola and long paved walk are not features enough for so large a garden. One kept getting distant views of brilliant colour and then coming slowly up to them. There was no element of surprise, no shock of beauty similar to the one I had experienced at Sissinghurst as we turned the corner and saw that great arc of white blossom from the *R. filipes* 'Kiftsgate' over the urn. It seemed to me we could do with some garden rooms as at Hidcote. Why not have the formalities of yew hedges, steps, balustrades, vases, fountains and different levels in an enclosure all of its own for the old-fashioned shrubs?

On the way home I thought of the genius of Gertrude Jekyll and Edwin Lutyens and the way they had planned the garden at Hestercombe in Somerset, the way the area she called 'the Great Plat' had been excavated on a flattish site, enclosed with short retaining walls and hedges and pergolas. I wanted a sense of period for the old roses. I did not want to re-create a part of La Malmaison but I did want stone and statuary. For these romantic old roses to stir my imagination it needed an atmosphere of bygone generations, and not the open spaciousness of a windy field. These roses need support—not wooden stakes, but brick walls and stone gilded with medallions of lichen. It was all too new-looking and vigorous and open—and we older gardeners do know that you can get an immense feeling of maturity in a garden after only fifteen years. Bone Hill is over twenty years old.

My last word of criticism—if opinion can be called criticism—is that with so much expertise evident in the growing, collection and selection of these old roses, it seemed a shame that while their physical well-being was being so well catered for, their artistic souls should be neglected, when more appropriate surroundings would have looked after these too. And we would all have benefited, in this age of the motor-bike exhaust and the screaming disco, from these quieter chords, brought by the roses whose very perfume and presence is balm from the immeasurable past.

L'envoi

The species roses, simple, single and elegant, are the work of nature—as I am a religious man, I am going to say the work of God. Cultivated roses as we know them—the old shrub roses and climbers of long ago, the sophisticated Hybrid Teas and Floribundas of today—are, as it were, the creation of man. How ever could he have been so successful? How could this stupid, muddling, inarticulate, greedy, envious, murderous, self-destructive, callous, cruel creature have managed to create out of his usual crass chaos so sweet and beautiful and tender an object as a rose? He has managed this. Perhaps the rest of his blundering civilization is nearer to flowering than we know—with music and pictures, literature and lovely gardens and architecture, the beautiful animals and plants he has bred—and especially the rose— are perhaps hopeful signs.

Photograph of 'Louis IV'.

Index

To help the reader, the index has been divided into two parts: an index of individual rose names, giving all the different species and varieties; and a general index. Variety names are usually put in quotation marks, but for ease of reading these have been left out in the index of rose names. The numbers in **bold type** refer to illustrations.

INDEX OF ROSE SPECIES AND VARIETIES

Agnes, 19, 91
alba semi-plena, **13**, 119
Albertine, 38, 80
Alchymist, 90, **91**, 105
Alexander, 106
Allen Chandler, 80
Aloha, 88, 118
Alpine Sunset, 106
Amelia, 105
Angela Rippon, 59
Anna Ford, 59
Anna Pavlova, 50
Apothecary's rose, 12, 16
arvensis, 23, 90
Ayrshire Splendens, 23

Baby Gold Star, 58
Ballerina, 43, **43**, 107, 121
banksiae lutea, 80
Baron Girod de l'Ain, 62, 68, 88
Baronne Adolphe de Rothschild, 69
Belle Amour, 105
Bennett's Seedling, 23
Blanc Double de Coubert, 19
Blue Moon, 47, 54, 64, 78, 79
Boule de Neige, 62, 67
Buff Beauty, 39
Burnet or Scots Briar, 39

californica plena, 88, **101**, 102, 103
Camphill Glory, 48, 50
Canary Bird, 39, 81, 121
Can-Can, 45
canina, 75
Capitaine John Ingram, 88, **89**, 103
Cardinal de Richelieu, 105
Celsiana, 11
centifolia muscosa, 66
    c.m. alba, 91
Cerise Bouquet, **102**, 103
Chanelle, 78, 79
Chaplin's Pink Companion, 99, 116, **116**,
    117
Charlotte Elizabeth, **116**
Chianti, 105
chinensis minima, 14, 57
    c. 'Viridiflora', 42, 59
Cinderella, 58
City of Leeds, 54, 85, 86, 87, 117
Climbing Cécile Brunner, 78, 79
Climbing Lady Hillingdon, 66, 80
Climbing Malaga, 96
Conditorum, 105
Constance Spry, **21**, 22, 80, 88, 96

Copenhagen, 96, 99
Cornelia, 10
Court Jester, 57
Cuisse de Nymphe Emue, 16
Cyril Fletcher rose, **71**, 74–5, 78, 79, 106,
    107

Daily Mail, 48
Danae, 10, 91
Darling Flame, 58
Dorothy Wheatcroft, 39
Dortmund, 116
Double Delight, **51**, 53
Dr W. van Fleet, 80
Dresden Doll, 58, 59
Duke of Windsor, 44, 45, 52
Dundee Rambler, 23
dupontii, 105
Dusty Maiden, 105
Dutch Gold, **51**

Eglantine, 23
Elizabeth Arden, 117
Empéreur du Maroc, 67
English Miss, 57
Erfurt, 117
Erinnerung an Brod, **14**
Ernest H. Morse, 12, 52, 80, 110
Esther's Baby, 59, **59**

Fairy, 121
Fairy Changeling, 42
Fairy Crystal, 42
Fairy Damsel, 42
Fairyland, 43
Fairy Moss, 58
Fairy Prince, 43
Fantin-Latour, 16, **18**, 88, 96, 119
Felicia, 10, **10**, 105
Félicité Parmentier, 88, **89**, 105, 119
Ferdinand Pichard, 62, 67, **68**, 119
Field rose, 23
filipes 'Kiftsgate', **9**, 10, 33, 69, 78, 79, 82,
    116, 122
Fisher Holmes, 105, **105**
F.J. Grootendorst, 88
foetida bicolor, 50
Fragrant Cloud, 45, 53, 106, 110, 118
La France, 19, 88
Francesca, 91
Francis Lester, **39**
Frühlingsgold, 39
Frülingsschnee, 121

gallica officinalis, 12, 16
Gillyflower rose, 42
Gloire de Ducher, 88
Gloire de Lawranceanas, 14
Gloire Lyonnaise, 91
Gloria Mundi, 58
Godfrey Winn, 47, 64
Golden Moss, 66, 91
Golden Showers, 78, 79, **89**, 91, 116
Goldfinch, 103
Grandpa Dixon, 47, 79, 80
Great Maiden's Blush, 16
Great Western, 88, **89**, 103
Green Diamond, 59
Green Ice, 59
Greensleeves, 54, 72
Gruss an Aachen, 43, 88

Hamburger Phoenix, 117, **120**
Handel, **46**
Harry Edland, 54
Helen Traubel, 95
Hunter, 117

Iceberg, 34, 45, 54, 78, 79, 86, 90, 117
Iced Ginger, 54, 86
Incense rose, 39, 69

Jacobite rose, 16
Josephine Bruce, 12, **46**, 79, 80, 86, 95
Just Joey, **51**, 53, 85, 86, 87, 99

Kathleen Harrop, 62, 68
Kazanlik rose, 14
King's Ransom, 52, 79, 80, 86
Königin von Danemarck, 119
Korresia, 54, **55**, 85, 86, 87, 117

Lady Johnson, 95, 99
Laneii (Lane's Moss), 78, 79
Lavender Lace, 59
Lavender Lassie, 103
lawranceana, 14
Lawrence Johnston, **31**, 117
Laxa, 75
Leverkusen, **104**, 105
Lilac Charm, 54, 85
Little White Pet, 90–1
longicuspis, 10, 33, 116
Louis IV, **123**
Louise Odier, 62, 68–9
Lovers Meeting, 118

macrantha, 105
Magenta, 19
Maigold, **112**, 116
Margaret Merril, 54, **55**, 72, 78, 79, 85, 86, 87
Max Graf, 42, **42**
May Queen, 66, 103
Mermaid, 80, 117
Midas, 47
Mme Alfred Carrière, 10, 78, 79
Mme Hardy, **113**, 119
Mme Isaac Pereire, 62, 66–7
Mme Louis Laperrière, 79, 80, 95
Mme Pierre Oger, 62, 67, 68
moschata plena, 103
Mountbatten, 45, **45**
Mousseline, 66
Mrs Anthony Waterer, 88, **89**, 103
Mrs John Laing, 62, 67
multiflora, 19, 75

Nevada, **21**, 22, 80
News, 54, **55**, 85–6, 87, 118
nitida, 42
Nozomi, 42, 58

Oakington Ruby, 58
Old Blush, 88
Old Velvet Rose, 118
Old Yellow Scotch, 68, 91

Papa Meilland, **7**, 12, 45, 50, **52**, 95
Parade, 116
Parkdirektor Riggers, 78, 79, 116
Pascali, 45
Paul's Himalayan Musk, 10, **32**, 103
Paul's Lemon Pillar, 10
Peace, 39, 52, 95
Peek-a-Boo, 42
Penelope, 10, 39, 78, 79
Peon, 58

Perle d'Or, 18, 102, 103, **104**, 105
Perpetual White Moss, 91
Phyllis Bide, 105
Piccadilly, 53
Pink Parfait, 57
Pink Perpètue, **33**
Pink Prosperity, 64
Pixie, 58
Président de Sèze, **61**, 118
Prima Ballerina, 45, 50, 52, 78, 79, 85, 86, 87, 110
primula, 39, 64, 69, 121
Prince Charles, 68
Prince Charlie's rose, 68
Princess Michael of Kent, 47
Pristine, 52

Quatre Saisons Blanc Mousseux, 91
Queen Elizabeth, 39

Raubritter, 42
Red Cascade, 58–9
Red Fountain, 117, **119**
Red rose of Lancaster, 16
Reine des Violettes, 62, 64–5
La Reine Victoria, 62, 67, 68, 88
Rob Roy, 54
Robusta, 116
Roger Lambelin, 18, 68
Rosa Mundi, 16, 67
Rose de Rescht, 103
Rose du Roi, 118
Roseraie de l'Hay, 39, **41**, 78, 79, 121
Rosina, 58
roulettii, **57**, 58
Royal Salute, 20
rubrifolia, 66, 121
rubus, 33
Rudolph Trimm, 72
rugosa, 75
  r. alba, 19, **38**, 39, 90, 121

Saga, 117
Sarah Van Fleet, 39
Scabrosa, 39
Scots Briar, 39
Seagull, **37**, 82, 106, 121
semperflorens, 18
Sheila's Perfume, 110
Silver Jubilee, **49**, 52, 106
Snow Carpet, 20, 40, 78, 79
Soleil d'Or, 19, 50
soulieana, 47
Souvenir de la Malmaison, 62, 69, 90, 102
Spinosissima, 91, 121
Starina, 58
Super Star, 45, 106

Temple Bells, 42
Thisbe, 10
Top Secret, 95
Troika, **51**, 78, 79, 80, 95, **97**, 99, 118
Tuscany, 10
Tuscany Superb, **6**, 54, 85
Typhoon, 46

Vanity, 105
Veilchenblau, 80
Vera Dalton, 116
Violette, 64
virginiana, 39
Vital Spark, 45

Wendy Cussons, 12, **51**, 53, 86, 95, **96**
Whisky Mac, 86, 106
White Cockade, 119
White rose of York, 16
William Lobb, 58, **65**, 66, 88, 121

Yesterday, 121

Zéphirine Drouhin, 62, **63**, 64, 80

GENERAL INDEX

Acaena 'Blue Haze', 46
Acer, 66
  A. palmatum atropurpureum, 66
  A. palmatum dissectum atropurpureum, 66
  A. platanoides 'Crimson King', 66
Aiton, William, *Hortus Kewensis*, 14
Ajuga, 44, 45
  A. reptans, 80
Alba roses, 8, 17, 88, **89**, 105, 119
  definition of, 16
Alchemilla mollis, 44
Alexandra, Queen, 113
The American Rose Annual (1979), 72
Anaphalis triplinervis, 44
  A. yedoensis, 62
Anthemis cupaniana, 64
Arches, 35
Asperula odorata, 44
Astell, Betty (Mrs Cyril Fletcher), 106
Aster novae-belgii, 62
Aster × frikartii, 44
Attar of roses, 14

Austrian Copper rose, 50
Ayrshire rose, 17
Azaleas, dwarf evergreen, 86

Bacon, Francis, 'Of Gardens', 66
Barrie, J.M., 66
Basil, 47
Beales, Peter, 50
Beech hedge, 23, 84
Bees of Chester 45, 70, 73, **74**, 74–5
  Sealand rose fields, 106, **107**
Benckendorff, Countess Sophie, 100
Berberis × stenophylla, 65
Blackspot, 28–9, **29**, 50, 58
Bone Hill (RNRS gardens and headquarters), St Albans, **31**, **37**, **41**, 42, 54, **55**, 85, 106, **109**, 110, 113–22
  displays of roses, 117–18
  pillar roses, 116–17
  pool and miniatures, 121
  Princess Mary Rose Walk, **109**, 121, 122
  reference library, 113

'Roses of Romance', 118–21
  trial grounds, 111
Bonemeal, 26–7
Bourbon roses, 17, 62, **63**, 64, 66–7, 68–9, 88, **89**, 90, 100, 103
  definition of, 18
Boursault roses, 17
  climbing, 17
Bowles, E.A., 60
Box hedges, 10, 44, 85
British Rose Growers' Association, 92
Brooke, Humphrey, 50, 69, 100, 102, **102**, 103, 105, 118
Budding, 75
Buddleia 'Lochinch', 47
Bugle, 44, 45
Burns, Robert, 6
Bush roses *see* Floribundas; Hybrid Teas

Campanula, 44
Camphill Village Trust, 50
Capital Radio gardens, 45, 113
  gazebo for, **36**

Capital Radio phone-ins, 32
Capsid bugs, 29
Caterpillars, 29
Ceanothus 'Gloire de Versailles', 62, 64, 65
Centifolia (or Cabbage) roses, 10, 17, 18, 43, 88, 119
  definition of, 16
Chafer beetle, 29
Charlemagne, 12
Chelsea Flower Show:
  1979, 36
  1980, 45, 113
  1981, 74, 86
China roses, 17, 91, 100
  definition of, 16, 18
  Hybrid, 100
Chives, 26, 44
Cineraria maritima, 44
Clematis, 30, 36–8, **39**, 65, 80
  C. cirrhosa balearica, 37
  C. Jackmannii, 37
  C. montana, 36
  C. patens 'Vyvyan Pennell', 37, 66
  C. tangutica, 37
  C. vitacella 'Etoile Violette', **39**
  C. × Jackmanii superba, 37
  'Duchess of Albany', 37
  'Gravetye Beauty', 37
  'Mme Edouard André', 37
  'Mrs Cholmondeley', 37
  rambler roses grown with, 36–8, **39**
Cleopatra, Queen, 12
Climbing roses, 17, 22, 30–8, **77**, 79, 81
  103, 116
  clematis grown with, 36–8, 65
  on fences, 34–5
  on house walls, **33**, 33–4, **35**
  miniature, 58–9
  pergolas, arches and porches, 35
  pruning, 28
  summerhouses and gazebos, 36, **36**
  trellis, 36
Cluster Roses *see* Floribundas
Cocker, J., 119
Concrete walls, pierced, for climbing roses, 36
Confucius, 12
Conifers, 44
  silver-leaved, 65
Container-grown roses, planting, 25
Convolvulus Cneorum, 46, 80
Correvon, Henry, 57
Cotinus coggygria 'Royal Purple', 66
Cotton lavender, 65
Cowper, William, 28
Creosote, 34
Crusaders, 12
Culpeper, 14
Curry plant, 65

Damask roses, 10, **11**, 12, 14, 17, 43, 105, **113**, 118, 119
  Autumn, 18
  definition of, 16
  Portland, 16, 17
Dead-heading, 28
Dictionary of Roses (Gault and Synge), 105

Diseases, 28–9
Dog roses, 11–12, 16, 30
Dot, Pedro, 58

Edging in the rose garden, 44, 47
Edland, Henry, Secretary of RNRS, 110
Elizabeth, Queen, the Queen Mother, 113
Elwes, E.V., 25, 26
Erigeron, 44

Feeding roses, 25–7
Fences, roses on, 34–5, **35**
Fertilizers, 26
Fish meal, 27
Floribunda (or Cluster) roses, 17, 20, 22, 34, 53–7, **55**, 72, 80, 81, 82, 83, 84, 85, 86, 90, 106, 122
  description of, 19, 53–4
  for hedges, 39
  pruning, 27, 28
Foliar feeding, 27
Forget-me-nots, 44, 100
Fuchsia magellanica 'Versicolor', 99
Furber, Robert, 'The Twelve Months of Flowers', 14

Gallica roses, 10, 12, 17, **61**, 85, 105, 118
  definition of, 16
The Gardener's Dictionary (1731), 14
Gardening catalogues, 22
  old, 14
Gault, S.M., 69, 105
Gazebos, 36, **36**
Geranium, 44
  'Johnson's Blue', **41**, 86
Gerard's *Herball*, 14
Gibson, Michael, 15
  Shrub Roses for Every Garden, 16
Golden marjoram, 47
Grass mowings, mulching roses with, 29
Great Dixter Gardens, 29
Greenfly, 26, 29
Gregory, Domini, 15
Gregory, Tony, 58, 82
Ground cover, 40–7, 80, 86
  roses for, 20, 40–2, 90

Hallows, Tony, **74**, 106
Harkness, J.L., 29, 42, 48, 50, 55, 59, 67, 72, 110, 118
  Roses, 73
Harvey, John H., 14
Heather, 43
Hebe pinguifolia pagei, 45–6
Hedges, roses for, 38–9
Helianthemum appeninum roseum, 46
Helichrysum italicum, 65
Henry Edland Memorial Medal (RNRS), 110
Herbs, used as ground cover, 44, 47
Hestercombe, Somerset, 122
Hidcote, 31, 64–5, 117, 122
Hilliers nursery, 42
Hole, Dean Reynolds, 108
Honey of roses, 14
Hosta, 45
  H. crispula, 45
  H. fortunei aurea, 45
  H. fortunei picta, 45

H. sieboldiana elegans, 45
  H. 'Thomas Hogg', 45
House walls, growing roses on, 33–4
Hyams, Edward, 47
Hybrid China roses, 100
Hybrid Musk roses, 10, **10**, 78, 91, 100, 103, 105
  definition of, 19
  for hedges, 39
Hybrid Perpetual roses, **14**, 17, 19, 62, 64–5, 67, 68, **68**, 69, 88, 91, 105, 118, 119
  definition of, 18
  in Lime Kiln Gardens, 100
Hybrid Polyantha roses, 19, 100
  see also Floribunda
Hybrid Tea roses, 17, 20, 22, 30, 32, 48–53, **51**, 72, 75, 80, 81, 82, 83, 84, 85, 86, 88, **93**, 95, 100, 106
  definition of, 19
  for hedges, 39
  pruning, 26–7, 27, 28
  yellow, 19, 50
Hydrangeas:
  climbing, 65
  lace-cap, 65
  mop-headed, 62
Hypericum, 117

Ivy, 30

Jekyll, Gertrude, 30, 69, 105, 122
Johnson, Hugh, 46
  Principles of Gardening, 52
Josephine, Empress, 14, 69

Kenwright, Terry, 74
Kew Gardens, 14
Kings Heath Park, Central TV Garden at, **21**, 99
Knossos, 12
Kordes, 58, 116
Kordes, R., 103
Kordes, Wilhelm, 103

Large Flowered Roses *see* Hybrid Teas
Lavender, 23, 65, 84, 85, 117
  Cotton, 44, 65
  dwarf, 44
Lawrance, Mary, *A Collection of Roses from Nature*, 14
Leafcutter bee, 29
Leaf-hoppers, 29
Leaf-miner, 29
Leaf-rolling sawfly, 29
Lilac, 65
Lilies, 81, 86, 100
Lilies-of-the-valley, 44
Lilium pyrenaicum, 69
Lime Kiln Gardens, 24, **32**, 69, 88, 100–105
Lindsay, Mrs Nancy, 42
Lloyd, Christopher, 29
London pride, 44
Lutyens, Edwin, 122

McGredy, Sam, 20, 40, 58, 78, 95, 97
  Look to the Rose, 40
MacLeod, Dawn, 42

La Malmaison, 14, 122
Manure, 24, 25, 26
Mawley, Edward, 108
Meilland, A., 50, 58
Mendel's theory, 72
Michaelmas daisies, 62
Mildew, 29
Miniature roses, 17, 20, 22, **56**, 57–9, **59**, 78, 81
  at Bone Hill, **114**, 121
  climbing, 58–9
  standard, 22, 58
Mint, variegated pineapple, 47
Modern Garden Roses, 17, 53
  see also Floribundas, Hybrid Teas
Modern Roses, 8, 72
Modern shrubs, 22, 53
Money, Keith, 50
Moore, Ralph, 58
Moss roses, 17, 66, 88, **89**, 91, 103, 121
  definition of, 16
  miniature, 58
Moyesii roses, 23
Mulching, 26, 29
Musk roses, 10, 18, 19, 23, 69
  Hybrid, 10, **10**, 19, 39, 78, 91, 100, 103, 105
Myrrh-scented rose, 23

Napoleon Bonaparte, 14
Nasturtium 'Red Roulette', 45
Nepeta, 44
Noisette, Philippe, 18
Noisette roses, 17, 18, 100
Nurserymen's catalogues, 14
Nymans, Sussex, 65

Ocimum basilicum, 47
Oil of roses, 12, 14
Old Garden Roses, 16–19, 53
  at Bone Hill, 116–17, **120**
  ground-cover among, 43–4
  at Lime Kiln Gardens, 100–105
  shrub roses, 22, 60–9
D'ombrain, Revd Honeywood, 108
Ophiopogon planiscarpus, 86
Origanum vulgare aureum, 47

Page, Courtney, 108, 110
Pansies, 44, 45, 80
Peat, 24
Pemberton, Revd Joseph, 10, 19, 23
Penzance briars, 38
Pereire, Anita, 100
Perfume industry, French, 12, 14
Pergolas, 35, **37**, 82, 116–17, 122
Perilla 'Atropurpurea Laciniata', 45
Pernet-Ducher, M., 19, 50
Petunias, 80
Phillips, Brigadier C.E. Lucas, 118
  Ornamental Shrubs, 67
Phloxes, 69
Phormium tenax purpureum, 66
Pillar roses, 22, **31**, 32, 67, 81, 97, 99, **112**
  at Bone Hill, 116–17, **120**
Pinks (*Dianthus*), 44
Plantain lily, 45
Planting, 23–5
  bare-rooted roses, 24–5

container-grown roses, 25
  near house wall, 34, **34**
  position, 23
  rose-sick soil, 24
  season, 23
  soil, 23–4
  standard rose, **25**
  tidying up rose bush before, **23**
Pliny, 12
Polyantha roses, 17, 19, 105
  Hybrid, 19, 100
  see also Floribundas
Porches, 35
Portland Damasks, 16, 17
Pot-pourri, 19
Poulsen, Niels, of Denmark, 19, 40
Price, Bob, 21, 99
Provence roses, 17
Pruning, **26**–7, 27–8, 44
  dead-heading, 28
Pullen, John, 115
Pyrus salicifolia pendula, 66

Queen Mary's Rose Garden, Regent's Park, 36, 82, 92–9

Rambler roses, 17, 19, 22, 30–8, 79, 81, 116
  on fences, 34–5
  growing clematis with, 36–8
  on house walls, **33**, 33–4
  pergolas, arches and porches, 35, **37**
  pruning, 28
  rooting, 42
  summerhouses and gazebos, 36
  in trees, 38–9
  trellis, 36
Red spider mite, 29
Redouté, Pierre-Joseph, 14, 18
Rock roses, 46
Romans, ancient, 12
Roper, Lanning, 100
Rosarians' Year Book, 108
Rose Annual (RNRS), 108, 110, 113
  1907 (first edition), 108
  1976, 25
  1977, 50, 52
  1980, 62, 72
Rose des Peintres, 16
Rose gardens, planning, 76–91
  average size, 78–80
  for an exposed site, 84
  large separate (Victorian), 85–7
  large separate (walled kitchen garden), 82, 83
  very small, 81
Rose hip syrup, 12
Rose leaves, crystallized, 16
Rose petal wine recipe, 15
Rose petals, some uses for, 12
Rose slugworm, 29
Rose tea, recipe, 16
Rose water, 12
Rosemary, 65
Roulet, Colonel, 57
Royal Horticultural Society, 108
Royal National Rose Society, 69, 92, 108–23
  awards, 110, 113

Bone Hill headquarters and gardens, **31**, **37**, 54, **55**, 85, 106, 109, **109**, 110, **111**, 113–22
Rose Annual, 25, 50, 52, 62, 72, 108, 110, 113
  trial grounds, 110, **111**
Rue, 47
Rugosa roses, 16, 24, 28, 78, 88, **89**, 90, 91, 100, 103, 117, 121
  definition of, 18–19
  for hedges, **38**, 39, **41**
Rust, 29

Sackville-West, Vita, 8, 10, 42, 60
Sage, 44
  grey, 47
  purple, 44, 47, 80
  tricolor, 47
  yellow variegated, 47
Salvia horminum (Clary) 'Bluebeard', 45
Salvia officinalis, 47
  S. o. icterina, 47
  S. o. purpurascens, 47
  S. o. tricolor, 47
Sangerhausen rose garden, 50
Santolina 44, 47, 80, 82, 85
  S. chamaecyparissus, 44, 65
Sargon, Sumerian king, 12
Saxifraga umbrosa, 44
Sedum, dwarf, 44
Select List of Varieties (RNRS), 108
Sempervirens roses, 17
Senecio laxifolius, 65
Sheridan, John, 110
Shrub roses, 79, 80, 82, 83, 92, 113, 121
  definition of, 22
  ground cover amongst, 43–4
  modern, 22, 39, 53, 80, 104, 118
  old, 22, 60–9, 84, 85, 86, 87, 96, 123
  pruning, 28
Shrubs, 65–6
Silver pear, weeping, 65
Sissinghurst, 8–10, 60, 122
  White Garden, **9**, 10
Soil, 23–4
  rose-sick, 24
Species roses, 28, 53, 103, 123
Specularia, Roman, 12
Sports, 30, 32
Spring bulbs, 80
Stachys lanata (Lamb's-lugs), 44, 46, **46**
Standard roses, 22, 81, 86
  half, 22
  miniature, 22
  planting, **25**
  pruning, 28
  weeping, 22, 36
Staples, Cliff, **107**
Stone, Christopher, 48
Strawberry, variegated, 46–7
Suckers, 28
Sugar of roses, 14
Summerhouses, 36
Sunken rose garden, 84
Suttons of Torquay, 45
Sweet briars, 10, 17, 23, 38, 39, 69
Sweet peas, 86
Sweet woodruff, 44
Synge, Patrick, 105